Wrong foot forward: US-Canada trade wars

DM Ole Kiminta

Published by KBros, 2025.

WRONG FOOT FORWARD: US-CANADA TRADE WARS

First edition. January 15, 2025.

ISBN: 978-1069109989

Written by DM Ole Kiminta.

Also by DM Ole Kiminta

How the Western Democracies failed the world
Supporting Refugees in their Homelands
Dissuading Global War Mongers:
Dissuading war mongers
La Libération Monétaire en Afrique
Canada Post: Management failure to modernise mail systems
Canada Post management failure to modernise mail systems
Canada Post: Management failure to modernise mail systems
Live to be 200
Aim to live for 200
Aim to live to be 200
Western democracies failed the world economies
Wrong foot forward: US-Canada trade wars
Canada begs to differ: Never a 51st state of USA

Table of Contents

Chapter 1: The impact of USA-Canada trade wars 1
Historical context of USA-Canada trade relations 3
The genesis of recent trade conflicts 5
Chapter 2: Economic Impacts 7
Job market disruptions 9
Effects on small businesses 11
Chapter 3: Tariffs on agricultural products 13
Impact on farmers and producers 15
Food prices and consumer choices 17
Chapter 4: Manufacturing and industry challenges 19
Supply Chain Disruptions 20
Fluctuating costs of production 22
Long-term Industrial consequences 24
Chapter 5: Consumer impact: 26
Availability of products 28
Changing consumer behaviour 30
Chapter 6: Impact of trade wars on environmental policies 32
Resource management challenges 34
Long-term sustainability issues 36
Chapter 7: Political ramifications 38
International relations and diplomacy 40
Public sentiment and civic engagement 42
Chapter 8: Potential resolutions and negotiations 44
Role of global trade agreements 46
The path forward 48
Chapter 9: Summary of key findings 50
Call to action for stakeholders 52
Vision for cooperative trade relations 54
Chapter 10: Unjustified borders 56
Historical Context of US-Canada Relations 58
Overview of trade wars and their implications 60
Chapter 11: The reality of illegal border crossings 62
Motivations behind illegal immigration 64

Case studies of notable border incidents 66
Chapter 12: The illicit drug trade 68
The impact of drugs on border communities 70
Policy responses to drug trafficking 72
Chapter 13: The flow of weapons across borders 74
The connection between drugs and weapons 76
Legal frameworks governing arms trade 78
Chapter 14: Economic implications of trade wars 80
The impact on bilateral trade 81
Consequences for local economies 83
The role of tariffs and trade agreements 84
Chapter 15: Diplomatic relations between the US and Canada 86
Current diplomatic challenges 88
The role of multilateral organisations 90
Chapter 16: Public perception and media representation 92
Case studies of media coverage 94
The role of social media in shaping narratives 96
Chapter 17: Alternatives to trade wars 98
Collaborative approaches to border security 99
Chapter18: Summary of key findings 103
Future directions for US-Canada relations 105
References 108

A note for the reader:

A recent remark made by an incoming American president about Canada becoming the 51st state of USA was taken lightly as a joke by many of us Canadians. However, the notion that we can avoid the incoming tariffs by accepting his "prudent" suggestion about our borders makes a surprisingly wild argument. The main reason for the friendly conversation emerged from the idea that we, the Canadians 'must do more to stop the illegal border crossing into USA, the flow of illicit drugs and weapons or face a tariff of 25% of what we sell to them. Although Canada has now invested more on border security, we all know that it is a terrible suggestion for both countries because border securities have almost nothing to do with legitimate trading. As for being a part of the USA, not many of us would entertain a thought on such matters.

Wrong foot forward: USA-Canada Trade wars

DM Ole Kiminta

The collapse of America's Free Trade consensus-origins (1935 signings- Roosevelt/ Mackenzie King)

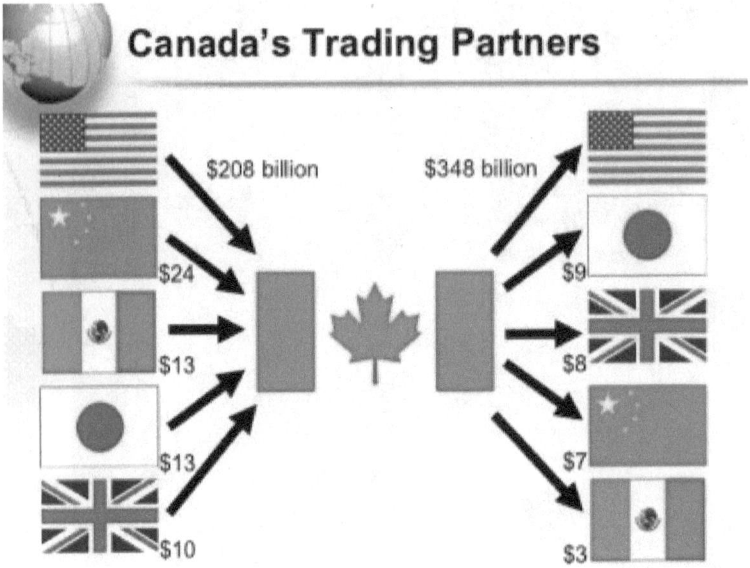
Canada's Trading Partners
$208 billion
$24
$13
$13
$10
$348 billion
$9
$8
$7
$3

Chapter 1: The impact of USA-Canada trade wars

The consequences of illegal border crossings and the flow of illicit drugs and weapons extend far beyond the immediate law enforcement challenges they present. Local economies, particularly those in border regions, face significant repercussions that can hinder growth and stability. When trade tensions escalate, as has been seen in recent years, local businesses often bear the brunt of these conflicts. The imposition of tariffs and trade barriers can lead to reduced access to markets, increased costs for consumers, and a general decline in economic activity within these communities. The consequences of illegal border crossings and the illicit flow of drugs and weapons cannot justify trade wars between the USA and Canada. The economic ramifications are far-reaching and detrimental to the very communities that such policies aim to protect. Policymakers must recognise the interconnectedness of local economies and work toward solutions that prioritise legitimate trade, community development, and cross-border cooperation rather than punitive measures that only serve to deepen economic divides. A focus on collaboration, rather than confrontation, will ultimately foster healthier economic environments and enhance the resilience of border communities.

Trade wars have become a prominent feature of international relations, particularly between nations with close economic ties, such as the United States and Canada. Understanding the dynamics of these trade wars is essential for grasping their implications on economies, industries, and consumers. A trade war typically involves the imposition of tariffs and other trade barriers by one country against another, aiming to protect domestic industries from foreign competition. In the context of the USA-Canada trade relationship, these conflicts can have wide-ranging consequences, affecting everything from agricultural exports to manufacturing and beyond.

At the heart of trade wars is the concept of protectionism, where governments seek to shield their domestic industries from foreign competition. In the USA-Canada context, this has often manifested in tariffs on goods like steel, aluminium, and agricultural products. The rationale behind imposing such tariffs is to support local businesses by making imported goods more expensive. However, this approach often leads to retaliation, where the affected country imposes its own tariffs, resulting in a cycle of escalating trade barriers that can harm both economies.

The ramifications of trade wars extend beyond immediate economic impacts. They can disrupt supply chains, increase costs for consumers, and lead to uncertainty in the market. For instance, Canadian businesses that rely on U.S. exports may face significant challenges when tariffs are imposed, leading to higher prices and reduced competitiveness. This not only affects businesses but also consumers who may find themselves paying more for everyday goods. Additionally, the uncertainty surrounding trade policies can deter investment, as companies may hesitate to commit to long-term plans in a volatile environment.

Moreover, trade wars often have social and political consequences. As industries suffer due to increased costs and lost markets, job losses can occur, leading to economic discontent. In both the U.S. and Canada, the public's reaction to trade wars can influence political discourse and policy decisions. Governments may feel pressured to take a firmer stance in negotiations or to implement measures to support affected workers and industries. This interplay between economics and politics can further complicate the resolution of trade disputes.

Understanding the intricacies of trade wars, particularly in the context of the USA-Canada relationship, is vital for recognising the broader implications of these conflicts. It is essential to consider not only the economic aspects but also the social and political dimensions that shape trade policies. As countries navigate these turbulent waters, the pursuit of mutually beneficial agreements becomes increasingly critical. The lessons learned from trade wars can inform future approaches to international trade, emphasising the need for cooperation and dialogue over conflict.

Historical context of USA-Canada trade relations

The historical context of USA-Canada trade relations is marked by a complex interplay of cooperation, competition, and conflict. From the early days of colonial trade to the formation of trade agreements, these relations have evolved significantly. Initially, trade between the two nations was informal and driven by geographical proximity. The British colonial era established significant trade routes, with goods flowing across the Great Lakes and the St. Lawrence River. This early commerce laid the groundwork for future economic ties, as both countries became intertwined through shared resources and interests.

The 19th century heralded a new era in trade relations, particularly following the War of 1812, which temporarily strained economic ties. However, the post-war period saw a resurgence in trade, leading to the Reciprocity Treaty of 1854, which reduced tariffs and expanded trade in specific goods. This agreement marked a pivotal moment, as it established a framework for bilateral trade that would influence future negotiations. The treaty's success demonstrated the mutual benefits of economic cooperation, setting a precedent for future agreements and fostering a sense of interdependence that would characterise USA-Canada relations for decades.

The emergence of industrialisation in both nations during the late 19th and early 20th centuries further intensified trade relations. As the United States became a manufacturing powerhouse, Canada served as a vital source of raw materials and a market for finished goods. The two nations began to recognise the importance of their economic relationship, leading to the establishment of the Canadian-American Reciprocal Trade Agreement in 1935, which aimed to reduce tariffs and promote trade during the Great Depression. This agreement signified a shift towards a more formalised and structured approach to trade, reinforcing the idea that economic partnership could lead to greater prosperity for both countries.

The post-World War II era brought significant changes to the global trade landscape, with Canada and the United States at the forefront of new economic initiatives. The General Agreement on Tariffs and Trade (GATT) in 1947 marked a commitment to reducing trade barriers globally, and both nations played active roles in this initiative. The establishment of the North American Free Trade Agreement (NAFTA) in 1994 further solidified their economic ties, eliminating tariffs on many goods and services. This agreement represented a culmination of decades of trade negotiations and cooperation, highlighting the importance of a stable and predictable trade environment for economic growth.

Despite the historically cooperative nature of USA-Canada trade relations, tensions have periodically arisen, particularly in response to changing political and economic landscapes. Trade wars, tariffs, and protectionist policies have emerged as significant challenges, often rooted in domestic political considerations rather than economic rationale. These conflicts have underscored the fragility of trade relations and the hidden costs associated with trade wars, affecting industries, consumers, and the broader economy in both nations. Understanding this historical context is crucial for recognising the complexities of current trade dynamics and the potential consequences of future conflicts.

The genesis of recent trade conflicts

The genesis of recent trade conflicts between the United States and Canada can be traced back to a complex interplay of economic, political, and social factors that have evolved over the years. The global landscape has shifted dramatically, with protectionist sentiments gaining momentum in various countries, including both the U.S. and Canada. This shift has been exacerbated by economic disruptions such as the 2008 financial crisis, which left many industries reeling and led to a re-evaluation of trade agreements and policies. The desire for self-sufficiency and national security has increasingly influenced trade discussions, fostering an environment ripe for disputes.

One of the primary catalysts for these conflicts has been the emergence of new trade policies aimed at prioritising domestic industries. In the United States, the administration's "America First" policy has led to a re-evaluation of longstanding trade agreements, including those with Canada. Tariffs imposed on steel and aluminium imports, often justified by national security concerns, have strained relations and prompted Canada to retaliate with tariffs of its own on various American goods. This tit-for-tat approach has not only affected bilateral trade but has also sent ripples throughout the broader North American economy.

Additionally, the rise of populism in both countries has further complicated trade relations. Leaders have capitalised on public discontent regarding job losses and economic inequality, framing trade as a key issue. In Canada, discussions surrounding the impact of U.S. tariffs have sparked debates about the vulnerability of certain sectors, such as agriculture and manufacturing. As both governments respond to domestic pressures, the focus on protecting local industries often takes precedence over collaborative trade solutions, leading to a cycle of escalation in conflicts.

The role of technological advancements and globalisation cannot be overlooked in this context. As supply chains have become increasingly integrated, the interdependence of the U.S. and Canadian economies has deepened. However, this interdependence has also made both nations more susceptible to the fallout from trade disputes. When tariffs are imposed, they not only affect bilateral trade but can disrupt supply chains that span multiple countries. This interconnectedness highlights the broader implications of trade conflicts, as they can lead to unintended consequences that impact consumers and businesses alike.

In conclusion, the recent trade conflicts between the United States and Canada are not isolated incidents but rather the result of a multitude of factors that have converged over time. Understanding the origins of these disputes requires a nuanced examination of economic policies, political dynamics, and social sentiments. As both nations navigate this challenging landscape, the costs of trade wars extend beyond simple tariffs and quotas, affecting industries, communities, and the overall economic stability of the region. Addressing these complexities will be crucial for finding pathways toward resolution and fostering a more cooperative trade environment in the future.

Chapter 2: Economic Impacts

Trade Balance and Economic Growth refers to the difference between a country's exports and imports of goods and services. It plays a crucial role in shaping a nation's economic landscape, influencing everything from currency strength to domestic production levels. A positive trade balance, where exports exceed imports, is often seen as an indicator of a healthy economy. Conversely, a negative trade balance, where imports surpass exports, can raise concerns about a country's economic stability. In the context of the USA-Canada trade wars, understanding the nuances of trade balance is crucial to grasping the broader implications for economic growth in both countries.

The trade relationship between the United States and Canada is deeply intertwined, with both countries relying on each other for a significant portion of their exports. Disruptions in this relationship, such as tariffs and trade restrictions, can lead to an imbalance that negatively affects economic growth. For instance, if Canada imposes tariffs on U.S. goods, it can result in reduced exports from the U.S. to Canada, which can subsequently affect jobs and production levels in American industries. Similarly, if U.S. tariffs lead to increased costs for Canadian imports, Canadian consumers may shift their purchasing behaviour, impacting domestic business revenues and economic activity.

Furthermore, trade wars can create uncertainty in the markets, leading businesses to delay investment decisions. When companies are unsure about future trade policies, they may refrain from expanding operations or investing in new technologies. This stagnation can have a ripple effect on innovation and productivity, two essential drivers of economic growth. In the long run, an unstable trade environment can hinder a country's competitive advantage in the global market, affecting its ability to sustain economic growth and job creation.

The impact of trade balance on economic growth is not limited to the immediate effects of tariffs and trade barriers. Long-term economic growth is fuelled by stable trade relationships that promote investment and collaboration. When countries engage in free trade, they can specialise in their competitive advantages, leading to increased efficiency and higher output. Trade wars disrupt this dynamic, forcing businesses to adapt to new realities that may not align with their strengths, ultimately resulting in slower economic growth.

In conclusion, the interplay between trade balance and economic growth is complex and multifaceted, especially in the context of the USA-Canada trade wars. The imposition of tariffs and trade restrictions can lead to immediate negative consequences on trade balances, which in turn can stifle economic growth. For policymakers and stakeholders in both nations, understanding this relationship is vital for devising strategies that promote sustainable economic development, ensuring that trade remains a positive force rather than a source of conflict.

Job market disruptions

Job market disruptions have emerged as a significant consequence of the USA-Canada trade wars, affecting industries, communities, and individual workers across both nations. As tariffs and trade barriers were imposed, businesses faced increased costs for raw materials and components, leading to a ripple effect throughout the economy. Many companies, particularly in manufacturing and agriculture, found themselves at a crossroads. With their profit margins squeezed, some opted to downsize their workforce, while others relocated production facilities to countries with more favourable trade conditions. This not only resulted in job losses but also contributed to a growing sense of uncertainty within the labour market.

The impact of these disruptions is particularly pronounced in regions heavily reliant on cross-border trade. Cities and towns that once thrived on the exchange of goods between the United States and Canada experienced sudden economic downturns as key employers laid off workers or closed their doors entirely. The fallout extended beyond immediate job losses; ancillary businesses, such as local suppliers and service providers, also faced declining revenues, leading to a cascading effect that further strained local economies. Communities that had benefited from stable employment opportunities now grappled with rising unemployment rates and diminished prospects for economic recovery.

Moreover, the trade wars have exacerbated existing disparities in the job market, particularly affecting marginalised groups. Workers in lower-wage industries, such as textiles and agriculture, often faced the brunt of layoffs, leading to increased economic insecurity. Additionally, those living in rural areas, where job options are typically limited, found it even more challenging to secure new employment opportunities. The ramifications of these disruptions have highlighted the vulnerability of certain segments of the workforce, drawing attention to the need for targeted support and retraining programs to help individuals transition into more stable jobs.

As the trade wars continue to unfold, the uncertainty surrounding future employment opportunities remains a pressing concern for many workers. The fear of further job losses or industry shifts has led to a more cautious approach to career planning and investment in skills development. Workers are increasingly seeking positions in sectors less susceptible to trade fluctuations, such as technology and renewable energy. However, the transition to these industries requires significant investment in education and training, which may not be readily accessible to all. This necessitates a comprehensive approach from both governments and educational institutions to equip the workforce with the skills needed to thrive in an evolving job market.

Ultimately, job market disruptions resulting from the USA-Canada trade wars serve as a stark reminder of the interconnectedness of global economies. The decisions made by policymakers can have profound implications for individuals and communities, underscoring the need for strategies that prioritise job stability and economic resilience. As both nations navigate the complexities of trade relations, it is essential to consider the long-term impacts on the workforce and to implement measures that foster sustainable employment opportunities for all citizens.

Effects on small businesses

The USA-Canada trade wars have far-reaching implications, particularly for small businesses that often lack the resources to absorb the shocks of increased tariffs and trade barriers. These businesses are essential components of the economy, providing jobs and fostering innovation. However, the volatility created by trade disputes can significantly disrupt their operations. Small businesses rely on predictable costs and stable supply chains, and when tariffs are imposed, they face rising costs for imported goods and materials, which can lead to higher prices for consumers and reduced competitiveness in the market.

Small businesses often operate on thin profit margins, making them particularly vulnerable to fluctuations in trade policies. Increased tariffs can lead to higher costs for raw materials, which can erode profits and force business owners to make difficult decisions regarding staffing, pricing, and investment in growth. Many small businesses may not have the financial cushion to absorb these costs, leading to a potential decrease in hiring or even layoffs. This creates a ripple effect throughout the local economy, as reduced spending by businesses translates to lower consumer confidence and spending.

In addition to direct financial impacts, small businesses also face challenges in navigating the complexities of changing trade regulations. The administrative burden of understanding and complying with new tariffs and import restrictions can be overwhelming for small business owners, who may not have dedicated legal or compliance teams. This can result in increased operational costs and a diversion of focus from core business activities, ultimately hindering growth and innovation. Furthermore, the uncertainty surrounding trade policies can stifle long-term planning, making it difficult for small businesses to invest in new projects or expand into new markets.

Consumer behaviour is also affected by trade wars, as rising prices due to tariffs can lead to decreased demand for certain products. Small businesses that rely heavily on imports may find themselves at a competitive disadvantage against larger firms that can better absorb increased costs or have diversified supply chains. When consumers face higher prices, they may prioritise spending on essentials, which can disproportionately impact small businesses that offer niche products or services. This shift in consumer behaviour can lead to a challenging environment for small businesses striving to maintain their market share.

Ultimately, the effects of USA-Canada trade wars on small businesses highlight the interconnectedness of local economies and international trade policies. While larger corporations may have the resources to weather these storms, small businesses often bear the brunt of such disruptions. As policymakers consider the implications of trade wars, it is crucial to recognize the vital role that small businesses play in economic stability and growth. Protecting these businesses through supportive policies and resources can help mitigate the adverse effects of trade disputes and foster a more resilient economic landscape.

Chapter 3: Tariffs on agricultural products

Tariffs on agricultural products have emerged as a contentious issue within the broader context of USA-Canada trade wars, significantly impacting both economies and the agricultural sectors of each country. These tariffs are taxes imposed on imported goods, and they are often employed as a tool to protect domestic industries from foreign competition. The agricultural sector, being a crucial part of both the American and Canadian economies, is particularly sensitive to such measures. Farmers and producers rely heavily on export markets, and any increase in tariffs can lead to higher prices, reduced demand for their products, and ultimately, financial strain.

In the context of USA-Canada trade relations, tariffs can disrupt established supply chains and create uncertainty for agricultural producers. For instance, when the United States imposed tariffs on Canadian dairy products, it not only affected Canadian dairy farmers but also impacted American consumers who faced limited choices and higher prices. This ripple effect illustrates the interconnectedness of the two markets. Tariffs can lead to retaliatory measures, wherein Canada may respond with its own tariffs on U.S. agricultural products, creating a cycle of escalation that harms both countries' agricultural sectors.

The implications of such trade barriers extend beyond immediate financial concerns. They can alter farming practices, forcing producers to adapt to a volatile market environment. Farmers may shift their focus to different crops or livestock that are less affected by tariffs, potentially leading to a decline in the diversity of agricultural production. Furthermore, the uncertainty generated by fluctuating tariffs can deter investment in the agricultural sector, as producers may be hesitant to commit resources to expand operations when future costs are unpredictable.

Another hidden cost of tariffs on agricultural products is the impact on rural communities. These communities often depend on agriculture as a primary source of income and employment. When tariffs lead to decreased profitability for farmers, the ramifications can be felt throughout the local economy. Businesses that support agriculture, such as equipment suppliers and processing facilities, may also suffer, leading to job losses and a decline in the overall economic vitality of rural areas. As a result, the consequences of trade wars extend far beyond the fields, affecting social structures and community cohesion.

Ultimately, the imposition of tariffs on agricultural products within the framework of USA-Canada trade wars reveals the complexities of international trade and its consequences. While intended to protect domestic interests, such measures can lead to unintended outcomes that harm both economies. Policymakers must carefully consider the broader implications of tariffs, recognising that the agricultural sector is not just a series of transactions but a vital component of the social and economic fabric of both nations. Balancing protectionist policies with the need for cooperation and mutual benefit will be essential for the future of U.S.-Canada trade relations.

Impact on farmers and producers

The trade wars between the USA and Canada have had significant repercussions for farmers and producers on both sides of the border. These agricultural stakeholders, who are pivotal to the economies of both nations, have faced a host of challenges stemming from tariffs, supply chain disruptions, and shifting market dynamics. The imposition of tariffs on goods such as dairy, poultry, and certain grains has not only raised costs for farmers but has also altered competitive landscapes, leading to uncertainty in long-term planning and investment.

Farmers in Canada have been particularly affected by tariff retaliations, which have targeted key agricultural exports. As the USA imposed tariffs on Canadian steel and aluminium, Canada responded with its own tariffs on American products, including certain agricultural goods. This back-and-forth has left Canadian producers grappling with reduced access to one of their largest markets. The dairy industry, for instance, has seen a decline in demand from American consumers, leading to oversupply issues in Canada and driving down prices for dairy farmers.

In the USA, farmers have also felt the brunt of the trade conflict. Many American agricultural producers rely heavily on exports to Canada, especially for crops like corn and soybeans. As trade tensions escalated, Canadian demand for these products diminished, resulting in surplus supplies and plummeting prices. The volatility in prices has made it challenging for farmers to maintain their livelihoods, leading to increased debt and financial instability in rural communities.

Moreover, the trade wars have disrupted established supply chains, complicating the relationships between producers and their suppliers. Farmers often depend on cross-border trade for essential inputs such as seeds, fertilizers, and equipment. Increased tariffs and regulatory restrictions have made these essential supplies more expensive and harder to obtain. This disruption not only affects the immediate costs for farmers but also hinders their ability to plan for future planting seasons.

The long-term consequences of the trade wars on farmers and producers extend beyond immediate financial impacts. The uncertainty surrounding trade policies has caused many agricultural stakeholders to reconsider their business strategies, with some exploring new markets or diversifying their crops. However, these adaptations come with inherent risks and require significant investment and time. In the end, the trade wars have not only altered the economic landscape for farmers and producers but have also raised questions about the sustainability of agricultural practices in an increasingly volatile trade environment.

Food prices and consumer choices

Food prices are a critical concern for consumers, directly influencing their purchasing decisions and overall economic well-being. The fluctuations in food prices can be attributed to various factors, including agricultural productivity, transportation costs, and international trade policies. In the context of the USA-Canada trade wars, tariffs and trade restrictions have exacerbated food price volatility, leaving consumers grappling with higher costs and limited choices. As these trade tensions persist, understanding their impact on food pricing becomes essential for consumers who must navigate an increasingly complex marketplace.

One significant consequence of the trade wars has been the imposition of tariffs on agricultural products. These tariffs often lead to increased costs for farmers and food manufacturers, which are ultimately passed on to consumers. For instance, tariffs on Canadian dairy products have resulted in higher prices for milk, cheese, and other dairy items in the United States. This not only affects the affordability of these essentials but also alters consumer buying habits, prompting many to seek alternatives or reduce their consumption of certain products.

Moreover, trade wars can disrupt established supply chains, leading to shortages and further price increases. The interdependence of the USA and Canada in the agricultural sector means that any disruption can have cascading effects. For example, delays at the border or restrictions on specific imports can limit the availability of fresh produce and other food items, driving up prices and forcing consumers to make difficult choices. This situation is particularly challenging for lower-income families, who may struggle to afford nutritious food options in the face of rising prices.

In addition to direct price impacts, trade wars can influence consumer perceptions and preferences. As individuals become more aware of the implications of trade policies, they may shift their purchasing decisions toward locally sourced or alternative products. This trend can lead to a greater emphasis on sustainability and food security, as consumers seek to support domestic agriculture and reduce reliance on imported goods. However, this shift may not always result in lower prices, as local products can sometimes be more expensive due to smaller production scales and higher operational costs.

Ultimately, the interplay between food prices and consumer choices is a reflection of the broader economic landscape shaped by trade policies. As the USA-Canada trade wars continue to unfold, consumers must remain vigilant and informed about how these developments impact their food costs and access to a diverse range of products. Understanding the underlying factors behind price fluctuations can empower consumers to make more informed choices, fostering resilience in the face of economic uncertainty and ensuring that they can continue to meet their nutritional needs.

Chapter 4: Manufacturing and industry challenges

Supply Chain Disruptions

Supply chain disruptions have become an increasingly prevalent issue in the context of the USA-Canada trade wars. These disruptions refer to the interruptions that affect the flow of goods and services from producers to consumers. When tariffs are imposed or trade agreements are renegotiated, businesses often face significant challenges in sourcing materials, managing inventories, and maintaining production schedules. The unpredictability of trade policies creates an environment where companies cannot rely on established supply chains, leading to delays, increased costs, and inefficiencies.

One of the primary factors contributing to supply chain disruptions is the imposition of tariffs. These taxes on imported goods can lead to increased prices for raw materials and components, forcing manufacturers to either absorb these costs or pass them on to consumers. For businesses that rely on cross-border trade between the USA and Canada, the uncertainty surrounding tariff rates can prompt them to seek alternative suppliers or production locations, disrupting established relationships and logistics. As a result, companies may experience longer lead times and reduced flexibility, ultimately affecting their ability to meet consumer demand.

Additionally, the trade wars have sparked a re-evaluation of supply chain strategies among companies operating in North America. Many businesses are now considering reshoring or nearshoring their operations to mitigate risks associated with dependence on global supply chains. This shift often involves significant investment in new facilities and workforce development within domestic markets. However, such transitions do not happen overnight and can lead to temporary inefficiencies and increased operational costs, further exacerbating supply chain disruptions during the adjustment period.

The impact of supply chain disruptions extends beyond individual businesses; it affects entire industries and the economy at large. Delays in production and distribution can lead to shortages of essential goods, impacting sectors such as automotive, agriculture, and consumer electronics. These shortages can create a ripple effect, driving prices up and limiting choices for consumers. Moreover, small and medium-sized enterprises may struggle to cope with these challenges due to their limited resources, which can further widen the gap between large corporations and smaller players in the market.

Finally, the long-term implications of ongoing supply chain disruptions resulting from the USA-Canada trade wars could reshape the landscape of North American trade. As businesses adapt to new realities, there may be a shift toward more localised supply chains that prioritise resilience over efficiency. This could lead to a reconfiguration of trade relationships, with an emphasis on building stronger partnerships within North America. While the immediate effects of supply chain disruptions are evident, the broader consequences will likely influence the future of trade policies and economic collaboration between the USA and Canada for years to come.

Fluctuating costs of production

Fluctuating costs of production play a critical role in shaping the economic landscape between the United States and Canada, particularly in the context of trade wars. These fluctuations can be attributed to various factors, including tariffs, supply chain disruptions, and changes in labour costs. As trade barriers are imposed or lifted, the costs associated with production can vary significantly, impacting businesses on both sides of the border. This volatility creates uncertainty for manufacturers and suppliers, ultimately affecting pricing strategies and consumer choices.

One major contributor to fluctuating production costs is the imposition of tariffs. When the U.S. or Canada imposes tariffs on imported goods, it raises the cost of raw materials and components for manufacturers relying on cross-border supply chains. For instance, a Canadian company that depends on U.S. steel may face higher prices due to tariffs, leading to increased production costs. This scenario forces companies to either absorb the costs, which can erode profit margins, or pass them on to consumers, potentially leading to higher prices for end products.

Additionally, the global supply chain is increasingly susceptible to disruptions caused by geopolitical tensions. Trade wars can lead to delays in shipping and increased costs associated with logistics. For example, if a manufacturer in Canada sources components from the U.S. and those components are delayed due to heightened customs checks or border restrictions, the production timeline is affected. Companies may need to seek alternative suppliers, which can be more expensive or less reliable, further driving up costs.

Labour costs also fluctuate in response to trade policies and economic conditions. In a trade war context, companies may struggle to find skilled labour due to heightened economic uncertainty. If businesses anticipate a downturn, they may freeze hiring or lay off workers, leading to a labour shortage when demand eventually rebounds. This mismatch can drive wages up, particularly in sectors that require specialised skills. As labour costs rise, companies must adjust their production strategies to maintain profitability, which can include investing in automation or relocating production facilities to regions with lower labour costs.

Ultimately, the fluctuating costs of production highlight the interconnectedness of the U.S. and Canadian economies. As trade wars continue to evolve, businesses must remain agile in their strategies to adapt to these changes. Understanding the implications of fluctuating production costs is essential for policymakers, business leaders, and consumers alike. By recognising these dynamics, we can better navigate the complexities of trade relations and make informed decisions that mitigate the hidden costs associated with trade wars.

Long-term Industrial consequences

The long-term industrial consequences of the USA-Canada trade wars extend far beyond immediate economic impacts. These conflicts have instigated a re-evaluation of supply chains, production strategies, and market access across various sectors. Industries that once thrived on cross-border collaboration now face uncertainty that disrupts established partnerships. As tariffs and trade barriers fluctuate, manufacturers become compelled to reconsider their dependency on shared resources, leading to a potential fragmentation of supply chains that can stifle innovation and efficiency.

One significant consequence of these trade wars is the potential for increased operational costs. Companies that previously benefited from the North American Free Trade Agreement (NAFTA) now encounter higher expenses due to tariffs on raw materials and finished goods. This shift not only affects profit margins but also leads to higher prices for consumers. Industries such as automotive and agriculture, which rely heavily on integrated supply chains, find themselves in precarious positions, potentially forcing them to relocate production facilities or seek alternative markets, thereby diminishing their competitive edge.

Moreover, the trade wars have prompted a reconsideration of labour markets in both countries. With companies facing increased costs, many may resort to downsizing or automating processes to maintain profitability. This can lead to job losses, particularly in sectors heavily reliant on cross-border trade. The ripple effect can impact local economies, resulting in reduced consumer spending and a decline in overall economic vitality. This shift not only alters the job landscape but also raises concerns about the skills gap, as workers in affected industries may need to retrain for emerging job markets.

Another long-term consequence is the potential erosion of trust between the USA and Canada. Trade wars breed animosity and suspicion, which can hinder future negotiations and cooperative efforts in other areas, such as environmental policy or security. A lack of collaboration may stifle progress in addressing shared challenges, such as climate change and technological advancements. As industries grapple with the repercussions of trade disputes, the broader implications for bilateral relations may lead to a more fragmented North American economy, limiting the potential for collective growth.

Lastly, the long-term impact on innovation cannot be overlooked. Trade wars create an environment of uncertainty that stifles investment in research and development. Companies may become risk-averse, opting to conserve resources rather than investing in new technologies or processes that could enhance productivity. This stagnation in innovation can hinder competitiveness on a global scale, as other nations continue to advance and capitalise on new opportunities. The resulting decline in technological advancement not only affects industries directly involved in trade but also has broader implications for the overall economic health of both the USA and Canada.

Chapter 5: Consumer impact:

Price increases and market choices

Price increases in the context of trade wars can have far-reaching effects on both consumers and businesses. When tariffs are imposed, the immediate consequence is often a rise in the cost of imported goods. In the case of the USA-Canada trade wars, these tariffs have led to increased prices for various products, from aluminium to agricultural goods. Consumers may find themselves paying more for everyday items, while businesses that rely on these imports face rising production costs. This scenario creates a ripple effect throughout the economy, as higher prices can lead to decreased consumer spending, ultimately stunting economic growth.

Market choices become increasingly limited as tariffs drive up prices and create barriers to trade. Domestic producers may struggle to compete with cheaper imports, leading to market consolidation and reduced options for consumers. In Canada, for example, certain sectors like dairy and poultry have been heavily protected, resulting in higher prices for local consumers compared to global markets. This lack of competition can stifle innovation and reduce the overall quality of goods available, forcing consumers to either accept higher prices or compromise on their choices.

The impact of price increases extends beyond mere economics; it also influences consumer behaviour. Faced with higher prices, consumers may alter their purchasing decisions, opting for cheaper alternatives or reducing their overall consumption. This shift can lead to a decline in brand loyalty, as shoppers prioritise affordability over quality or brand reputation. As consumers navigate these changes, they may turn to local products, which, while potentially more expensive, may offer a sense of supporting local economies. However, this can also create a false sense of security, as the underlying issues of price inflation and market imbalance remain unresolved.

For businesses, the challenge of operating in a high-tariff environment requires strategic adjustments. Companies may be compelled to absorb increased costs, pass them onto consumers, or seek alternative sourcing strategies. This can lead to a re-evaluation of supply chains, potentially shifting operations to countries with more favourable trade agreements. While this may mitigate some immediate effects of price increases, it also introduces complexities related to supply chain management and quality control. Companies must balance the need for cost reduction with the imperative to maintain product integrity and customer satisfaction.

Ultimately, the interplay between price increases and market choices reveals the intricate consequences of trade policies. Policymakers must recognise that their decisions can significantly impact consumer behaviour and market dynamics. To foster a healthy economic environment, it is crucial to consider the long-term implications of tariffs and trade wars on both consumers and businesses. A nuanced understanding of these relationships is essential for fostering a resilient economy that can withstand the pressures of international trade disputes while ensuring that consumers are not left bearing the brunt of increased costs.

Availability of products

The availability of products in the context of USA-Canada trade wars has emerged as a significant concern for consumers and businesses alike. Trade disputes often lead to tariffs and trade barriers, which can disrupt supply chains and create shortages. This is particularly evident in industries heavily reliant on cross-border trade, such as agriculture, automotive, and technology. As tariffs increase the cost of imported goods, companies may scale back production or seek alternative suppliers, resulting in fewer options for consumers.

The agricultural sector illustrates the complexities of product availability during trade tensions. Canadian farmers, for instance, depend on the U.S. market for a substantial portion of their exports. When tariffs are imposed on Canadian agricultural products, such as dairy and poultry, it not only affects the income of Canadian farmers but also alters the availability of these products in both countries. Consumers may face higher prices or find certain items missing from grocery store shelves, leading to a ripple effect throughout the food supply chain.

In the automotive industry, the impact of trade wars can be particularly pronounced. Many vehicles are manufactured using parts sourced from both the U.S. and Canada. Trade disputes can lead to disruptions in supply, as manufacturers may find it more expensive or logistically challenging to import necessary components. This can result in production delays and, ultimately, fewer vehicles available for sale. The consequences extend to consumers who may experience limited choices and increased prices as manufacturers pass on the costs associated with tariffs.

The technology sector also suffers from trade tensions, as many electronic products are produced using a complex web of international suppliers. The imposition of tariffs can lead to increased costs for manufacturers, who may choose to limit production or delay the launch of new products. This can hinder innovation and access to the latest technology for consumers, who may find themselves waiting longer for new devices or facing higher prices for existing products. The interconnected nature of technology supply chains means that disruptions can have far-reaching effects on product availability.

Ultimately, the availability of products during trade wars highlights the interconnectedness of the U.S. and Canadian economies. Consumers in both countries benefit from a diverse range of goods made possible by cross-border trade. However, when trade tensions arise, the resulting barriers can lead to product shortages, increased prices, and diminished choices. Understanding the implications of these trade wars is crucial for consumers, policymakers, and businesses as they navigate the complex landscape of international trade and its impact on everyday life.

Changing consumer behaviour

Changing consumer behaviour in the context of the USA-Canada trade wars has become a crucial area of study for understanding the broader implications of these economic conflicts. As tariffs and trade barriers are imposed, consumers begin to adapt their purchasing habits in response to changing prices and the availability of goods. This shift is not merely a reaction to higher costs; it reflects a deeper transformation in consumer attitudes and perceptions regarding domestic and foreign products. Understanding these changes is essential for businesses, policymakers, and economists looking to navigate the complexities of the trade environment.

One significant aspect of changing consumer behaviour is the increased focus on local goods. With trade tensions rising, many consumers have begun to prioritise products made in their own country. This shift can be attributed to a growing sense of nationalism and a desire to support local economies. As a result, Canadian consumers may avoid American products not just due to price increases but also as a political statement. This trend can impact sales for companies that heavily rely on cross-border trade, forcing them to adapt their marketing strategies to highlight their domestic connections.

Moreover, consumers are becoming more informed and conscientious about the origins of their purchases. The trade wars have highlighted the vulnerabilities in global supply chains, prompting consumers to scrutinise where their products come from and the ethics behind their production. There has been a noticeable rise in demand for transparency and sustainability, with consumers increasingly seeking brands that align with their values. This shift means that businesses must evolve to provide clearer information about their supply chains and the social and environmental impact of their goods.

The economic uncertainty created by the trade wars has also led to a more cautious consumer base. As consumers worry about potential job losses, inflation, and the overall stability of the economy, their spending habits become more conservative. This change can result in decreased discretionary spending and a pivot towards essential goods and services. Retailers and manufacturers must recognise this shift and adapt their inventory and marketing strategies accordingly to maintain consumer engagement and loyalty.

The rise of e-commerce and digital platforms has empowered consumers to access a wider range of products, often at more competitive prices. As consumers increasingly turn to online shopping, the impact of trade wars is amplified by the ability to compare prices and product origins effortlessly. Businesses must leverage these digital tools to reach consumers effectively, ensuring they communicate the value of their products in a landscape where consumer loyalty can be fleeting. Understanding these dynamics is vital for navigating the challenges posed by the evolving trade landscape between the USA and Canada.

Chapter 6: Impact of trade wars on environmental policies

Trade wars, particularly those between the United States and Canada, have significant repercussions that extend beyond economic metrics. One of the most concerning impacts is on environmental policies. In the quest to protect domestic industries, governments often prioritise short-term economic gains over long-term environmental sustainability. This shift can lead to weakened regulations and a reduction in funding for environmental initiatives, ultimately compromising efforts to combat climate change and protect natural resources.

As tariffs and trade barriers rise, industries may push for more lenient environmental regulations to reduce operational costs. The competitive pressure to maintain profit margins can lead to a race to the bottom, where environmental protections are sacrificed in favour of economic survival. This phenomenon is particularly evident in sectors like manufacturing and energy, where companies may lobby for exemptions from environmental standards, arguing that compliance would hinder their ability to compete effectively against foreign entities.

Moreover, the uncertainty generated by trade wars can disrupt collaborative international efforts aimed at addressing environmental challenges. Research and conservation initiatives often rely on cross-border cooperation, which can be jeopardised by political tensions. When nations become preoccupied with protecting their own interests, as seen during trade conflicts, the collective action necessary for tackling global issues such as climate change and biodiversity loss tends to decline. This retreat from collaboration can stall progress on international environmental agreements.

The impact of trade wars on environmental policies is also felt at the local level. Communities that depend on natural resources for their livelihoods may find themselves caught in the crossfire. For instance, increased tariffs on imported goods can lead to a rise in domestic production, often in environmentally sensitive areas. This can result in habitat destruction, increased pollution, and depletion of local ecosystems, as businesses prioritise quick returns over sustainable practices. As a consequence, the social contract between industries and communities regarding environmental stewardship may erode.

Ultimately, the intersection of trade wars and environmental policies reveals a complex dynamic that necessitates careful consideration. While the immediate economic implications of trade conflicts are often front and centre in public discourse, the long-term environmental consequences may be more insidious. As policymakers navigate the turbulent waters of international trade, it is crucial to integrate environmental sustainability into the conversation, ensuring that efforts to protect domestic industries do not come at the expense of the planet's health.

Resource management challenges

One of the primary challenges in resource management is the fluctuation of prices due to trade barriers. Tariffs can lead to increased costs for raw materials, forcing companies to either absorb these costs or pass them on to consumers. This unpredictability makes it difficult for businesses to plan their budgets and investment strategies. Industries heavily reliant on specific imports, such as steel or softwood lumber, have been particularly hard hit. The resulting price volatility not only strains companies but also disrupts the market equilibrium, leading to ripple effects that extend beyond individual businesses.

Moreover, the trade wars have prompted many companies to reconsider their sourcing strategies. Some firms have sought to localise production to mitigate the risks associated with international trade. While this approach can enhance supply chain resilience, it also poses challenges in terms of resource availability and labour costs. Companies must navigate the complexities of sourcing materials domestically, which may not always be feasible or cost-effective. This shift can lead to a scarcity of certain resources, further complicating the landscape of resource management amidst trade tensions.

Environmental considerations also play a role in the resource management challenges stemming from trade disputes. The increased focus on local sourcing can sometimes lead to over-exploitation of domestic resources, raising concerns about sustainability. As companies pivot to meet immediate needs, the long-term implications for the environment and resource conservation are often sidelined. This creates a paradox where efforts to stabilise supply chains may inadvertently contribute to environmental degradation, highlighting the need for a balanced approach to resource management.

Finally, the ongoing uncertainty surrounding trade policies complicates strategic planning for businesses. The potential for further escalations in trade disputes means that companies must remain agile and adaptable. This necessity can divert attention and resources away from innovation and growth initiatives, as businesses focus on short-term survival strategies. The challenge lies not only in managing immediate resource needs but also in anticipating future developments in trade relations. A proactive approach that incorporates flexible resource management strategies is essential for navigating the complexities introduced by the USA-Canada trade wars.

Long-term sustainability issues

The trade tensions have disrupted established supply chains and have led to increased costs for businesses. These disruptions can result in inefficiencies that compromise the long-term viability of industries that rely on cross-border trade. As companies struggle to adapt to fluctuating tariffs and trade barriers, their ability to invest in sustainable practices diminishes, which ultimately affects the broader economy and the environment.

The agricultural sector, a critical component of both the U.S. and Canadian economies, has faced particular strain due to trade disputes. Farmers have become increasingly reliant on exports to support their operations, and trade wars have led to retaliatory tariffs that hurt their market access. This situation not only threatens the livelihoods of farmers but also impacts food security and sustainability. An unstable trade environment can discourage investment in sustainable agricultural practices, as farmers may prioritize short-term financial survival over long-term ecological health.

Moreover, the manufacturing sector has also shown signs of vulnerability due to trade conflicts. Companies that once enjoyed seamless access to both markets now grapple with increased production costs and uncertainty. This instability can lead to diminished innovation in sustainable manufacturing practices, as businesses may focus more on immediate operational challenges rather than long-term investment in cleaner technologies. The shift toward sustainability in manufacturing is critical for reducing carbon footprints and addressing climate change, yet trade wars can stifle these necessary advancements.

The environmental implications of trade wars are also significant. As countries engage in protectionist policies, they may inadvertently promote less sustainable practices. For instance, the reliance on local production to counteract trade barriers can lead to a rise in pollution and resource depletion if companies prioritise quantity over sustainability. Furthermore, trade wars can hinder international cooperation needed to tackle global environmental challenges, such as climate change, where collaboration is essential for developing effective solutions.

Ultimately, the long-term sustainability issues arising from the USA-Canada trade wars necessitate a re-evaluation of trade policies. Policymakers must consider the broader implications of their decisions, ensuring that trade agreements promote not only economic growth but also environmental stewardship and social responsibility. A sustainable approach to trade will foster resilience in industries, support farmers and manufacturers in their transition to greener practices, and contribute to a more stable economic future for both nations. Addressing these issues will be crucial in mitigating the hidden costs of trade wars and securing a sustainable path forward.

Chapter 7: Political ramifications

Domestic political landscape

The domestic political landscape in both the United States and Canada plays a pivotal role in shaping the dynamics of trade relations between the two countries. As economic interdependence deepens, political decisions increasingly reflect the complexities of trade policies and their implications for domestic constituencies. In both nations, trade policies are often influenced by lobbying groups, public sentiment, and regional interests, which can lead to significant variations in how trade issues are prioritized. Understanding this landscape is crucial to grasping the broader implications of the USA-Canada trade wars.

In the United States, the political discourse surrounding trade has shifted significantly in recent years. A growing faction within the Republican Party has embraced a more protectionist stance, arguing that free trade agreements often disadvantage American workers. This shift has been accompanied by a rise in populism, which has altered the traditional bipartisan consensus on trade. As politicians respond to the concerns of their constituents, particularly in manufacturing-heavy regions, policies that prioritise protectionism over cooperation have emerged. Such political trends have direct consequences for trade relations with Canada, leading to increased tensions and retaliatory measures.

Canada, on the other hand, has maintained a generally open stance towards trade, viewing strong ties with the United States as essential for its economic well-being. However, domestic political pressures have also shaped Canada's approach to trade negotiations. The Liberal government, while advocating for free trade, faces challenges from opposition parties that question the benefits of certain agreements and call for more stringent protections for Canadian industries. As public opinion fluctuates in response to the perceived impacts of trade wars, Canadian leaders must balance international commitments with domestic expectations, which can complicate negotiations with their American counterparts.

The impact of trade wars is not limited to economic metrics; it also reverberates through social and political channels. In both the U.S. and Canada, communities that rely heavily on cross-border trade often find themselves caught in the crossfire of political posturing. This can lead to heightened tensions among local businesses, workers, and government officials, as each group seeks to advocate for their interests. The result is a fragmented political landscape where consensus on trade policies becomes increasingly elusive. As the public becomes more aware of these complexities, calls for more transparent and inclusive trade discussions are likely to grow.

Ultimately, the domestic political landscape in both the United States and Canada is a crucial factor in understanding the ongoing trade wars. As leaders navigate the intricate web of local interests, public opinion, and international obligations, the potential for missteps increases. The consequences of these trade wars extend beyond the immediate economic impacts, influencing social cohesion and political stability in both nations. Recognising the interplay between domestic politics and trade policy is essential for stakeholders seeking to mitigate the hidden costs associated with these conflicts.

International relations and diplomacy

International relations and diplomacy between the United States and Canada have historically been defined by a complex interplay of cooperation and tension. The economic relationship between the two nations is one of the most significant in the world, characterised by deep trade ties, shared cultural values, and mutual strategic interests. However, trade wars can strain this relationship, revealing underlying vulnerabilities that can have cascading effects on diplomacy. The repercussions of trade disputes extend beyond immediate economic impacts, influencing political alliances, security cooperation, and cross-border community ties. Understanding these dynamics is essential for grasping how trade tensions can reshape diplomatic relations.

The USA-Canada trade relationship is built on a foundation of agreements such as the North American Free Trade Agreement (NAFTA), now replaced by the United States-Mexico-Canada Agreement (USMCA). These agreements have facilitated the movement of goods, services, and labour across borders, fostering economic interdependence. However, when disputes arise—whether over tariffs, regulatory standards, or trade imbalances—the diplomatic fabric can fray. The imposition of tariffs can lead to retaliatory measures, escalating tensions that complicate negotiations on other fronts, such as environmental policy, security cooperation, and immigration. This interconnectedness underscores how trade wars can undermine broader diplomatic efforts.

The diplomatic fallout from trade wars can also impact public perception and national identity. In both countries, trade disputes may fuel nationalist sentiments, prompting calls for protectionism and a re-evaluation of long-standing partnerships. Politicians may exploit these sentiments for electoral gain, framing trade wars as necessary for national sovereignty, even at the cost of international cooperation. This shift in public opinion can challenge the long-term stability of bilateral relations, as citizens become more polarised and sceptical of the benefits of trade agreements. The resulting atmosphere can hinder constructive dialogue, making it difficult for diplomats to navigate complex issues that require collaborative solutions.

Furthermore, trade wars can have significant implications for regional stability and security. The United States and Canada share a robust security partnership, exemplified by joint military initiatives and intelligence sharing. However, when economic tensions rise, the focus on mutual security may wane. Distrust can seep into other areas of cooperation, undermining efforts to address common threats such as climate change, terrorism, and cyber security. The notion that economic competition can lead to geopolitical rivalry complicates the ability of both countries to maintain a united front in international forums, ultimately affecting their global standing and influence.

In conclusion, the intersection of international relations and diplomacy in the context of USA-Canada trade wars reveals a complex landscape where economic disputes can ripple through political and social spheres. The consequences extend far beyond financial markets, impacting public sentiment, national security, and regional stability. As both nations navigate the challenges posed by trade tensions, it is crucial to recognise the importance of diplomacy in mitigating conflicts and fostering cooperation. Understanding these dynamics is essential for policymakers and citizens alike, as they seek to navigate the hidden costs of trade wars and work towards a more stable and mutually beneficial relationship.

Public sentiment and civic engagement

Public sentiment plays a crucial role in shaping the landscape of civic engagement, particularly in the context of the USA-Canada trade wars. As trade tensions escalate, public opinion often reflects a complex interplay of economic concerns, national identity, and regional interests. In both countries, citizens grapple with the potential ramifications of tariffs and trade barriers on their day-to-day lives. This growing awareness can lead to heightened civic engagement, as individuals seek to understand the implications of trade policies and advocate for their interests.

In Canada, public sentiment regarding the USA-Canada trade wars has been influenced by a deep-rooted reliance on American markets. Many Canadians worry about job losses and the impact on industries such as agriculture and manufacturing, which are particularly vulnerable to changes in trade policy. This anxiety has prompted increased participation in civic activities, including town hall meetings, public forums, and social media campaigns aimed at influencing policymakers. As citizens become more informed about the intricacies of trade agreements, their engagement often translates into collective action, reflecting a desire to protect domestic interests.

Conversely, in the United States, public sentiment surrounding trade wars often mirrors broader political divides. While some Americans view protective tariffs as necessary for safeguarding domestic jobs, others argue that such measures lead to higher consumer prices and strained international relations. This polarisation can complicate civic engagement, with individuals aligning their views along partisan lines. However, grassroots movements have emerged, driven by a shared concern over economic stability and job security. These movements strive to mobilise citizens across political affiliations, emphasising the importance of cross-border cooperation and mutual economic benefit.

Platforms like Twitter and Facebook have become vital tools for disseminating information and mobilising support for various causes related to the trade wars. Advocacy groups and concerned citizens utilise these platforms to share personal stories, raise awareness about the consequences of trade policies, and call for legislative action. As discussions unfold online, they often spill over into real-world activism, further blurring the lines between digital engagement and traditional forms of civic participation.

Ultimately, the relationship between public sentiment and civic engagement in the context of the USA-Canada trade wars highlights the importance of informed citizenship. As individuals become more aware of the issues at stake, their engagement can influence policy decisions and foster a sense of community. Encouraging dialogue and collaboration across borders is essential for addressing the challenges posed by trade conflicts. By understanding the hidden costs of these wars, citizens can advocate for policies that promote economic resilience and mutual prosperity, ensuring that their voices are heard in the ongoing discourse surrounding trade relations.

Chapter 8: Potential resolutions and negotiations

Potential resolutions and negotiations surrounding the USA-Canada trade wars require a nuanced understanding of the economic and political landscapes that have shaped these relations. Trade disputes often arise from a combination of tariffs, regulatory barriers, and differing standards that can create significant friction between the two nations. To address these issues effectively, both countries must engage in comprehensive dialogues that prioritize mutual benefits over unilateral gains. By identifying common ground, both governments can lay the groundwork for sustainable solutions that protect their economic interests while fostering a spirit of cooperation.

One viable resolution could involve renegotiating existing trade agreements, like the United States-Mexico-Canada Agreement (USMCA). This renegotiation process could address specific grievances related to tariffs and quotas that have generated tension. A thorough review of these agreements, with input from stakeholders across various sectors, can help to identify areas where adjustments may be needed. By involving industry representatives and labour organisations in the discussions, both governments can ensure that the needs of the workforce and businesses are adequately represented, leading to more equitable outcomes.

In addition to renegotiations, establishing a bilateral trade commission could serve as a platform for ongoing dialogue. This commission would be tasked with monitoring trade relations, assessing the impacts of policies, and facilitating communication between the two governments. By creating a formal structure for negotiations, Canada and the USA can address issues proactively rather than reactively. This approach could help prevent misunderstandings and conflicts before they escalate into more significant trade wars, ultimately benefiting both economies.

Another potential resolution involves leveraging multilateral forums, such as the World Trade Organization (WTO), to mediate disputes. By bringing trade issues to an international platform, both countries can benefit from third-party insights and recommendations. This strategy not only encourages adherence to global trade norms but also demonstrates a commitment to resolving conflicts through established frameworks. Engaging with other nations within these forums can foster a sense of accountability and transparency, promoting fair trade practices that are crucial for long-term economic stability.

Finally, fostering public and private partnerships can enhance the effectiveness of negotiations. Collaboration between governments, businesses, and civil society can lead to innovative solutions that address the root causes of trade tensions. By promoting joint ventures and initiatives that highlight the interdependence of the USA and Canada, both nations can build stronger economic ties that reduce the likelihood of future conflicts. Public awareness and support for these initiatives are essential, as a well-informed citizenry can advocate for policies that prioritise collaboration over competition, ultimately leading to a more harmonious trade relationship.

Role of global trade agreements

Global trade agreements play a crucial role in shaping the economic landscape between countries, particularly in the context of the USA-Canada trade relationship. These agreements are designed to facilitate trade by reducing tariffs, eliminating trade barriers, and fostering a more predictable trading environment. In the case of the United States and Canada, trade agreements such as the North American Free Trade Agreement (NAFTA), which has now been replaced by the United States-Mexico-Canada Agreement (USMCA), have significantly influenced bilateral trade flows, economic growth, and job creation. Understanding the implications of these agreements is essential to grasping the broader impact of trade wars.

The negotiation and implementation of global trade agreements are often complex processes that require careful consideration of the interests of various stakeholders. In many instances, these agreements aim to balance the needs of domestic industries with the benefits of free trade. However, when trade wars erupt, such as between the USA and Canada, these agreements can become points of contention. Tariffs and other trade barriers can disrupt established trade patterns, leading to increased costs for consumers and businesses. This disruption highlights the fragility of trade relations and the importance of maintaining strong agreements that promote stability.

Trade agreements also encompass provisions related to labour, environmental standards, and intellectual property rights, which can have far-reaching implications for both countries involved. For instance, the USMCA includes updated labour provisions designed to improve working conditions in Mexico, thereby addressing concerns about wage disparities that affect Canadian and American workers. Such measures can be seen as essential for ensuring that trade benefits are equitably distributed. However, when trade disputes arise, these provisions may be threatened, undermining the progress made in previous negotiations.

Moreover, global trade agreements can serve as a platform for diplomatic engagement, fostering closer ties between countries. The collaborative nature of trade negotiations can enhance mutual understanding and cooperation, which are vital in times of tension. When trade wars escalate, the breakdown of dialogue can exacerbate conflicts and hinder efforts to resolve underlying issues. This aspect of global trade agreements underscores their role not only as economic tools but also as instruments of foreign policy.

In conclusion, the role of global trade agreements in the context of USA-Canada trade wars is multifaceted. They provide a framework for economic cooperation, establish essential standards, and facilitate diplomatic relations. However, the hidden costs of trade wars reveal the vulnerabilities inherent in these agreements. As the two nations navigate the complexities of their trade relationship, the lessons learned from past agreements and conflicts will be crucial in shaping a more resilient and equitable approach to international trade in the future.

The path forward

The path forward in the context of the USA-Canada trade wars necessitates a comprehensive understanding of the underlying issues that have driven tensions between these two neighbouring countries. As both nations grapple with the economic repercussions of tariffs, trade barriers, and retaliatory measures, it becomes increasingly crucial to explore strategies that could foster a more collaborative trade relationship. The first step involves recognising the interconnectedness of the economies, where trade policies in one country significantly influence the other. By acknowledging this interdependence, stakeholders can begin to see the value in pursuing solutions that prioritise mutual benefits over competitive isolation.

A critical component of moving forward is the need for dialogue between policymakers, industry leaders, and trade organisations in both countries. Establishing open lines of communication can facilitate a better understanding of each country's economic priorities and concerns. Regular summits and joint forums could serve as platforms for discussing trade challenges and exploring cooperative solutions. Engaging with diverse voices from various sectors, including agriculture, manufacturing, and technology, will ensure that the perspectives of all affected parties are considered, thereby creating a more inclusive approach to trade negotiations.

Furthermore, addressing the hidden costs of trade wars is essential for paving a sustainable path forward. These costs often manifest in the form of higher consumer prices, disrupted supply chains, and reduced market access for businesses. To mitigate these effects, both governments should consider implementing policies that minimize tariffs and other trade barriers while promoting fair competition. A focus on long-term trade agreements that emphasise stability and predictability can help restore trust and confidence among businesses and consumers alike, fostering an environment conducive to economic growth and cooperation.

Innovation and investment in technology can also play a pivotal role in redefining the trade landscape between the USA and Canada. By harnessing advancements in digital trade, both countries can create new opportunities that transcend traditional trade barriers. Collaborative efforts in sectors such as clean technology, artificial intelligence, and e-commerce can lead to groundbreaking partnerships that enhance competitiveness on the global stage. Encouraging cross-border investments in research and development will not only benefit individual companies but also strengthen the overall economic resilience of both nations.

Ultimately, the path forward lies in a commitment to building a more equitable and sustainable trade relationship. By focusing on collaboration, open communication, and shared goals, the USA and Canada can work together to navigate the complexities of the global economy. Emphasising the importance of strategic partnerships will allow both nations to address the challenges posed by trade wars while reaping the benefits of a united front. This cooperative spirit can lay the groundwork for a prosperous future, where both countries thrive in harmony, ensuring that the lessons learned from past conflicts guide their collective progress.

Chapter 9: Summary of key findings

The trade wars between the United States and Canada have revealed a complex web of interdependencies that significantly impact both nations. One of the key findings is the economic strain caused by tariffs and trade barriers. These measures, designed to protect domestic industries, often backfire, leading to increased costs for consumers and businesses alike. As companies face higher input costs, they may pass these expenses onto consumers, resulting in inflationary pressures that erode purchasing power. The ripple effects extend beyond immediate price hikes, influencing investment decisions and economic growth prospects in both countries.

Another critical finding is the disruption of supply chains that has occurred as a result of the trade wars. The close economic ties between the U.S. and Canada have facilitated the establishment of integrated supply chains over the years. However, the imposition of tariffs has forced companies to reevaluate their sourcing and production strategies. Many have sought alternative suppliers outside the North American region, which can lead to longer lead times and increased logistical complexities. This shift not only affects the industries directly involved but also creates a broader impact on employment and economic stability in both nations.

The social implications of the trade wars are also noteworthy. As communities reliant on cross-border trade experience job losses and economic decline, social cohesion may fray. The resulting economic uncertainty can exacerbate disparities within regions, leading to increased tensions and dissatisfaction among the populace. This discontent can manifest in various forms, from protests to political mobilisation, as communities seek solutions to the challenges posed by the trade conflict. The social fabric of both countries is thus at risk, as the fallout from trade policies extends beyond economic metrics into the realm of public sentiment and community well-being.

Environmental considerations have emerged as another key area impacted by the trade wars. As companies shift production to avoid tariffs, there may be unintended consequences for sustainability efforts. The relocation of manufacturing processes can lead to increased carbon footprints if firms move operations to countries with less stringent environmental regulations. Furthermore, the focus on short-term economic gains may overshadow long-term commitments to green initiatives, complicating efforts to address climate change. The trade wars, therefore, represent not only an economic challenge but also a potential setback in the pursuit of environmental sustainability.

Finally, the trade wars highlight the need for a re-evaluation of trade policies and their broader implications. Policymakers must recognise that the interconnectedness of the U.S. and Canadian economies necessitates a more collaborative approach to trade. Rather than resorting to protectionist measures, fostering cooperation and dialogue could yield mutually beneficial outcomes. This shift in perspective could help mitigate the adverse effects of trade conflicts, promoting economic resilience and stability in both countries. Ultimately, the findings underscore the importance of understanding the intricate dynamics of trade relationships and the necessity for policies that promote long-term prosperity over short-term gains.

Call to action for stakeholders

First and foremost, businesses operating in both countries must engage in advocacy for fair trade practices. This involves actively participating in dialogues with government representatives and industry associations to highlight the specific impacts of trade tariffs and restrictions on their operations. By sharing insights and data on lost revenue, disrupted supply chains, and reduced competitiveness, businesses can help inform policy decisions that prioritize equitable trade agreements. Moreover, companies should explore alternative markets and diversify their supply chains to mitigate risks associated with potential future trade disruptions.

Policymakers play a crucial role in shaping the trade landscape and must prioritise collaboration over confrontation. They should engage in constructive negotiations aimed at resolving existing disputes while establishing frameworks that prevent future conflicts. This includes revisiting existing trade agreements, such as the United States-Mexico-Canada Agreement (USMCA), to ensure they reflect the current economic realities and address the concerns of all stakeholders. Additionally, policymakers should invest in trade education and outreach to help businesses understand their rights and the available resources for navigating trade challenges.

Consumers, too, have a vital role to play in this call to action. By becoming informed about the implications of trade wars on product availability and pricing, consumers can make conscious purchasing decisions that support local industries and promote fair trade practices. Engaging with brands that prioritize ethical sourcing and production can drive demand for goods that are produced under fair conditions, thereby influencing companies to adopt more responsible practices. Furthermore, consumers should advocate for policy changes that support international cooperation and trade fairness, ensuring their voices are heard in the political arena.

Lastly, stakeholder collaboration is essential for fostering resilience in the face of ongoing trade tensions. Establishing coalitions among businesses, trade associations, and consumer groups can amplify efforts to address shared concerns and advocate for systemic change. By pooling resources, knowledge, and influence, these coalitions can effectively lobby for policies that promote sustainable trade practices, support domestic industries, and protect workers' rights. The time for stakeholders to unite and take proactive steps is now, as the future of USA-Canada trade relations hinges on collective action and a commitment to fostering mutual prosperity.

Vision for cooperative trade relations

The vision for cooperative trade relations between the United States and Canada is rooted in the understanding that both nations share a deep economic interdependence. This relationship is not only significant for economic growth but also for maintaining stability in North America. By fostering a cooperative framework, both countries can work towards eliminating trade barriers, enhancing supply chain resilience, and ensuring that their economies are better equipped to face global challenges. A collaborative approach can lead to mutually beneficial agreements that prioritise fairness and equity, benefiting industries and consumers alike.

One of the primary components of this vision is the establishment of transparent and consistent trade policies. Clear guidelines can help businesses on both sides of the border navigate regulations without fear of sudden changes that can disrupt operations. By engaging in dialogue and negotiation, the two nations can address existing trade disputes and set a precedent for resolving future conflicts amicably. This proactive approach not only mitigates the risk of trade wars but also reinforces a commitment to shared economic goals.

Collaborative initiatives, such as joint research projects and investment in infrastructure, can create a more integrated market that leverages the strengths of both economies. By pooling resources and expertise, the United States and Canada can address pressing issues like climate change and supply chain vulnerabilities more effectively. This cooperative spirit can turn challenges into opportunities, showcasing the power of collaboration.

Education and workforce development also play a crucial role in this vision. As industries evolve, both countries must ensure that their workforce is prepared to meet new demands. Joint training programs and educational exchanges can help develop a skilled labour force that is capable of thriving in a competitive global market. By investing in human capital, the U.S. and Canada can strengthen their economic ties while fostering a culture of cooperation that transcends borders.

Finally, a vision for cooperative trade relations must include a commitment to inclusivity and fairness. Trade agreements should consider the needs of all stakeholders, including small businesses and marginalised communities. By ensuring that the benefits of trade are widely shared, both countries can create a more equitable economic landscape. This inclusive approach will not only strengthen bilateral relations but also promote a sense of shared responsibility and partnership that can withstand the test of time, ultimately contributing to the long-term prosperity of both nations.

Chapter 10: Unjustified borders

The Concept of borders in modern trade

The concept of borders in modern trade has evolved significantly in response to globalisation, technological advancements, and shifting political landscapes. While traditional notions of borders emphasise physical barriers that delineate national territories, contemporary trade practices often transcend these boundaries. The rise of free trade agreements and regional economic collaborations has blurred the lines that once strictly defined national markets. As a result, the interaction between countries, especially the United States and Canada, has fostered economic interdependence that challenges the justification for imposing trade wars based on illicit activities.

Illegal border crossings, particularly those associated with the flow of drugs and weapons, have become focal points in discussions about national security and trade policy. However, it is vital to recognize that these illegal activities do not reflect the broader economic relationship between the two nations. The U.S. and Canada share one of the most extensive trading partnerships in the world, with billions of dollars exchanged daily in legitimate goods and services. The complexities of this relationship cannot be simplified to the actions of a minority engaged in unlawful practices, as the majority of cross-border interactions are beneficial and lawful.

Moreover, the impact of trade wars initiated under the pretext of combating illegal activities can have far-reaching consequences on legitimate businesses and consumers. Tariffs and other trade barriers can disrupt supply chains, inflate prices, and hinder economic growth. For example, industries reliant on cross-border collaboration, such as automotive manufacturing and agriculture, face significant challenges when political tensions escalate into trade disputes. The resulting economic instability disproportionately affects ordinary citizens and small businesses that depend on smooth trade relations for their livelihoods.

In addition to economic implications, the narrative surrounding borders in modern trade must also consider the social and cultural ties that exist between nations. The United States and Canada share a long history of cooperation and mutual benefit, characterized by shared values and common interests. These cross-border connections extend beyond commerce, encompassing cultural exchanges, familial ties, and academic collaborations. Ignoring these aspects in favour of a narrow focus on border enforcement and trade wars undermines the foundational relationship that has developed over decades.

Ultimately, addressing the complexities of borders in modern trade requires a nuanced understanding of the factors at play. While it is crucial to combat illegal activities that threaten public safety and economic stability, equating these issues with the broader context of U.S.-Canada trade relations overlooks the substantial benefits of collaboration. A more effective approach would involve enhancing diplomatic efforts, investing in joint initiatives to tackle illicit trade, and maintaining open channels for legitimate commerce that foster prosperity for both nations.

Historical Context of US-Canada Relations

The historical context of US-Canada relations is marked by a complex interplay of trade, diplomacy, and security concerns that have evolved significantly over the centuries. Initially, the relationship was shaped by colonial legacies and territorial disputes. After gaining independence, both nations sought to solidify their borders and establish trade relationships that would enhance their economic viability. The Treaty of Paris in 1783, which ended the American Revolutionary War, delineated boundaries that would become critical in shaping the future interactions between the two countries. Over time, these early agreements laid the foundation for a partnership defined by mutual interests in trade, economic growth, and regional stability.

The 19th century witnessed significant developments in US-Canada relations, particularly with the expansion of railroads and the establishment of new trade routes. The Corn Laws in Britain and the subsequent repeal in 1846 shifted economic dynamics, prompting Canada to seek closer economic ties with the United States. The Reciprocity Treaty of 1854 allowed for duty-free trade in various goods, fostering a period of economic interdependence. However, this period was not without tension, as issues related to border security and immigration policies began to emerge. The influx of immigrants into both countries, particularly during the Gold Rush, highlighted the need for more structured immigration and border control policies.

The emergence of the 20th century brought new challenges and opportunities for US-Canada relations, particularly in the context of two World Wars. During World War I and World War II, the two nations collaborated closely, both militarily and economically. The establishment of the Ogdensburg Agreement in 1940 formalized cooperation on defence matters, leading to the creation of the Permanent Joint Board on Défense. This cooperation set a precedent for future collaborative efforts and reinforced the idea that security concerns would often intertwine with trade and diplomatic relations. The post-war period saw the signing of the General Agreement on Tariffs and Trade (GATT), further integrating the economies of the two countries.

By the late 20th century, US-Canada relations were characterised by significant trade agreements, most notably the Canada-United States Free Trade Agreement (CUSFTA) in 1989, which paved the way for the North American Free Trade Agreement (NAFTA) in 1994. These agreements aimed to eliminate trade barriers and foster economic cooperation, contributing to an unprecedented level of cross-border trade. However, the rise of globalisation and the increasing flow of illicit drugs and weapons across the border began to complicate the narrative. As illicit activities intensified, they raised questions about security and trade that threatened to overshadow the longstanding partnership.

In the contemporary context, the challenges posed by illegal border crossings and the flow of drugs and weapons have sparked debates about the justification for trade wars between the two nations. While these issues are undeniably significant, they should not overshadow the historical cooperation and interdependence that have defined US-Canada relations. The emphasis on security should ideally be balanced with the recognition of the mutual benefits derived from trade and diplomacy. A focus on collaboration rather than confrontation can help address the complexities of border security while preserving the economic ties that have long been a hallmark of the relationship between the United States and Canada.

Overview of trade wars and their implications

Trade wars represent a significant escalation in economic tensions between nations, often characterised by the imposition of tariffs and other trade barriers. The ongoing trade disputes between the United States and Canada illustrate how economic policies can become intertwined with broader geopolitical concerns. Factors such as the flow of illicit drugs and weapons across borders have fuelled national security rhetoric, leading to trade measures that may ultimately harm both economies. Understanding the implications of these trade wars provides insight into the complexities of international relations and the interconnectedness of trade, security, and diplomacy.

One of the primary drivers of trade wars is the perception of unfair trade practices. In the case of the U.S.-Canada relationship, accusations of subsidisation, dumping, and other forms of economic manipulation have led to calls for protective measures. These actions are often justified by claims of protecting domestic industries and securing national interests. However, such justifications frequently overlook the reality that trade wars can exacerbate the very issues they aim to address, such as illegal border crossings and the trafficking of illicit drugs and weapons, thereby undermining the security objectives they purport to support.

The implications of trade wars extend beyond immediate economic impacts, affecting diplomatic relations and regional stability. The U.S.-Canada trade relationship has historically been characterized by cooperation, yet trade wars can create an environment of distrust and hostility. This shift can hinder collaborative efforts to combat transnational issues, including drug trafficking and border security. When nations engage in economic hostilities, they may become less willing to share intelligence or work together on joint security initiatives, ultimately making them more vulnerable to the very threats they seek to mitigate.

Moreover, trade wars can have dire consequences for ordinary citizens. Increased tariffs often lead to higher prices on imported goods, which can disproportionately affect lower-income populations. As the cost of living rises, public sentiment may turn against the government's trade policies, particularly when these policies are seen as a response to illegal activities rather than a well-considered economic strategy. The detrimental effects on consumers can further complicate the political landscape, making it harder for policymakers to navigate the delicate balance between trade and security.

In conclusion, the overview of trade wars highlights their multifaceted implications, particularly in the context of U.S.-Canada relations. While concerns regarding illegal border crossings and the flow of illicit drugs and weapons are valid, using these issues to justify trade wars may lead to counterproductive outcomes. Instead of fostering security, such measures can damage economic ties, hinder diplomatic relations, and ultimately undermine the very goals they aim to achieve. A more nuanced approach that considers the complexities of trade, security, and international cooperation is essential for addressing the challenges posed by illicit activities without resorting to destructive economic conflicts.

Chapter 11: The reality of illegal border crossings

Statistics and trends in border crossings between the United States and Canada reveal a complex landscape influenced by a variety of factors, including economic conditions, immigration policies, and law enforcement practices. Data from the Department of Homeland Security and the Canada Border Services Agency indicate that despite fluctuations in cross-border travel due to events such as the COVID-19 pandemic, the overall trend in recent years has been a gradual increase in both legal and illegal crossings. For instance, in 2022, there were over 400,000 apprehensions for illegal crossings along the U.S.-Canada border, highlighting a significant concern for authorities on both sides. This figure is notable when compared to previous years, suggesting a shift in patterns that merits further exploration.

The flow of illicit drugs and weapons across the border has been a critical factor in shaping the policies and perceptions surrounding border security. Recent statistics show that while the majority of goods and individuals crossing the border are legitimate, a concerning percentage involves the trafficking of drugs, particularly opioids such as fentanyl. Law enforcement agencies have reported an increase in drug seizures, indicating that traffickers are exploiting loopholes in the border system. This trend creates a narrative that often oversimplifies the complexities of cross-border trade and leads to calls for stricter measures that could inadvertently impact legitimate trade relations.

Moreover, the economic implications of heightened border security measures cannot be overlooked. The U.S.-Canada trade relationship is one of the largest and most integrated in the world, with billions of dollars exchanged in goods and services daily. An analysis of trade statistics reveals that over 75 percent of Canadian exports go to the United States, emphasizing the interconnectedness of the two economies. The introduction of more stringent border controls in response to concerns about illicit crossings could disrupt this flow, potentially leading to trade wars that harm both nations. The consequences of such actions could be detrimental, particularly in sectors heavily reliant on cross-border supply chains.

Public perception of border crossings is heavily influenced by media narratives that often exaggerate the dangers posed by illegal crossings and drug trafficking. This skewed representation can lead to a public outcry for increased security measures, overshadowing the reality that the vast majority of cross-border activities are benign. Data indicates that most individuals crossing the border do so for legitimate reasons, such as work, tourism, or family visits. Misunderstanding the statistics can create a false sense of urgency, prompting policymakers to implement drastic measures that may not be justified by the available evidence.

In summary, the statistics and trends in border crossings between the U.S. and Canada reflect a nuanced reality that challenges simplistic narratives linking illegal activities to trade tensions. While concerns about drug trafficking and illegal crossings are valid, they should not serve as a basis for justifying trade wars that could have far-reaching negative impacts on both economies. A more balanced approach that recognises the importance of legitimate trade and the interconnectedness of the two nations is essential for fostering a stable and prosperous relationship. Addressing the underlying issues of border security should focus on collaboration and evidence-based policies rather than punitive measures that could jeopardise long-standing trade ties.

Motivations behind illegal immigration

Illegal immigration is a complex phenomenon driven by a myriad of factors that extend beyond mere economic motivations. One of the primary motivations behind illegal immigration is the pursuit of better economic opportunities. Individuals from countries with high unemployment rates or stagnant economies often seek to migrate to nations like the United States, where they perceive a higher potential for financial stability and growth. This quest for improved living conditions can compel individuals to undertake significant risks, including crossing borders without authorisation, in hopes of securing a better future for themselves and their families.

In addition to economic factors, social and political instability in home countries plays a crucial role in driving illegal immigration. Many individuals flee violence, persecution, or oppressive political regimes, seeking refuge and safety in more stable environments. For these migrants, the decision to cross borders illegally may stem from a genuine need for protection and human rights, highlighting the humanitarian aspect of the issue. This necessity for safety often overshadows the legal ramifications they face, as the urgency of their circumstances compels them to prioritise immediate survival over adherence to immigration laws.

Another significant motivation is the influence of established immigrant communities in destination countries. Family reunification drives many illegal immigrants to cross borders, as individuals seek to join relatives who have already settled in places like the United States or Canada. The presence of these communities can create a network of support that eases the transition for newcomers, providing them with resources and information that facilitate their integration. This social dynamic not only perpetuates the cycle of illegal immigration but also underscores the deep-rooted connections that exist across borders, which can be overlooked in broader discussions about immigration policies.

Economic disparities between countries can also lead to a flow of illicit goods, including drugs and weapons, which intersect with the motivations behind illegal immigration. While some individuals may be drawn to illegal activities as a means of survival, others may find themselves caught in a cycle of exploitation, where their immigration status leaves them vulnerable to criminal organisations. This intertwining of illegal immigration with the drug trade and organised crime complicates the narrative, suggesting that the motivations behind illegal border crossings are often multifaceted and deeply interwoven with broader socio-economic issues.

Addressing the motivations behind illegal immigration requires a nuanced understanding that goes beyond the simplistic notion of border enforcement. Policymakers must consider the underlying factors that drive individuals to risk their lives in search of better opportunities, safety, and community. By recognising the complexities of illegal immigration, stakeholders can work towards more effective and humane solutions that address the root causes rather than merely the symptoms of this pressing issue. This holistic approach is essential in fostering dialogue around immigration policies, particularly in the context of trade relations and the impact of illicit activities on bilateral agreements.

Case studies of notable border incidents

Border incidents between the United States and Canada have often highlighted the complexities of international relations, trade, and security. While the two nations share one of the longest and most peaceful borders in the world, notable incidents have tested diplomatic ties and raised questions regarding border policy. These case studies illustrate how issues like illegal border crossings and the flow of illicit drugs and weapons can impact bilateral relations, often leading to heightened tensions that threaten economic collaboration.

One significant incident occurred in 2017 when the U.S. witnessed a surge in asylum seekers crossing from Canada into states like Vermont and New York. Many of these individuals were fleeing unstable conditions in their home countries, seeking refuge under U.S. immigration laws. The situation drew attention to the inadequacies of existing border policies and sparked debates about whether these crossings should be treated as a humanitarian issue or a violation of border security. This incident prompted discussions around the Safe Third Country Agreement, which governs the movement of refugees between the two nations and raised concerns about how trade relations could be affected by the changing landscape of immigration enforcement.

Another notable case was the 2020 seizure of a significant shipment of fentanyl and other illicit drugs at the U.S.-Canada border. While the majority of cross-border trade is legitimate, the interception of these harmful substances underscored the ongoing struggle against drug trafficking. Law enforcement agencies in both countries collaborated to address this growing concern, emphasizing the importance of joint efforts in combating drug-related crime. However, the incident also served as a catalyst for political discourse, with some factions arguing that increased border security measures were necessary, potentially threatening the free trade agreements that have long benefited both economies.

In 2021, a series of high-profile firearms trafficking cases drew attention to the flow of weapons across the border. Investigations revealed that firearms originally purchased in the U.S. were being smuggled into Canada, where they fuelled organized crime and violence. These incidents highlighted the vulnerabilities in border security and prompted discussions about the impact of such crimes on public safety. The implications for trade were significant, as calls for stricter border controls risked undermining the cooperative spirit that has characterised U.S.-Canada relations. The case illustrated that while national security is a priority, it cannot come at the expense of economic collaboration and shared interests.

Lastly, the 2022 border blockade involving truckers protesting vaccine mandates showcased how domestic issues can spill over into international relations. The protests led to significant disruptions in trade, particularly affecting supply chains between the two countries. While the protestors aimed to challenge health policies, the blockade brought to light the vulnerabilities of cross-border trade infrastructure. The incident raised concerns about how internal dissent could lead to broader economic implications and strained relationships, reinforcing the notion that border incidents should be carefully navigated to maintain the balance between security and trade.

Chapter 12: The illicit drug trade

Drug trafficking networks are complex and multifaceted systems that operate across international borders, exploiting vulnerabilities in law enforcement, economic disparity, and social conditions. These networks are often characterised by their ability to adapt and evolve in response to law enforcement efforts, utilising advanced technology and sophisticated logistics to transport illicit substances. Understanding the structure and function of these networks is essential for grasping the broader implications of drug trafficking on trade relations, particularly between countries like the USA and Canada.

At the core of drug trafficking networks are various actors, including producers, traffickers, distributors, and street-level dealers. Each group plays a distinct role in the supply chain, with producers typically located in regions where the cultivation of illicit drugs is prevalent, such as rural areas in Mexico or Colombia. Traffickers then transport these drugs across borders, often using established smuggling routes and methods that take advantage of porous borders. This progression from production to distribution underscores the global nature of drug trafficking, as it is not confined to a single country or region but rather spans continents and involves a myriad of stakeholders.

The financial incentives associated with drug trafficking are significant, often motivating individuals and organised crime groups to engage in these illegal activities. The revenue generated from the sale of illicit drugs can be astronomical, leading to the proliferation of violence and corruption in communities where these networks operate. This economic impact extends beyond the borders of the countries involved, as the drug trade can destabilise entire regions, challenge law enforcement agencies, and create public health crises that demand international attention and resources.

Moreover, the relationship between drug trafficking and trade policies is increasingly scrutinised, particularly in the context of U.S.-Canada relations. While both nations share a long border and strong economic ties, the flow of illicit drugs and weapons can strain diplomatic relations and result in calls for stricter border controls and trade restrictions. However, using drug trafficking as a justification for trade wars overlooks the complexities of the issue and the need for cooperative strategies that address the root causes of trafficking, such as poverty, lack of education, and social inequality.

To effectively combat drug trafficking, it is crucial for countries to work together through intelligence sharing, law enforcement collaboration, and comprehensive policy approaches that address both demand and supply. Diplomatic efforts should focus on fostering partnerships that enhance security without resorting to punitive measures that may exacerbate existing tensions. The fight against drug trafficking must be framed within a broader context of global trade and diplomacy, recognising that unilateral actions may not yield the desired outcomes and could inadvertently harm legitimate economic relations.

The impact of drugs on border communities

The impact of drugs on border communities is a multifaceted issue that encompasses social, economic, and security dimensions. In areas along the U.S.-Canada border, the presence of illicit drug trafficking has significantly altered the dynamics of local communities. These regions often serve as transit points for drugs entering the United States from Canada, leading to increased criminal activity and the destabilisation of local economies. The consequences of this illicit trade extend beyond mere law enforcement challenges, affecting public health, community cohesion, and overall quality of life.

Economically, border communities that grapple with drug trafficking face unique challenges. The presence of illegal drug trade can deter legitimate business investments, as potential investors may perceive these areas as high-risk environments. Local businesses often suffer from reduced patronage due to crime and safety concerns, leading to job losses and economic decline. Furthermore, the diversion of law enforcement resources to combat drug-related activities can detract from community development initiatives, leaving these areas struggling to thrive in an increasingly competitive economic landscape.

Socially, the impact of drugs permeates the fabric of border communities, affecting families and individuals on multiple levels. The prevalence of substance abuse can lead to increased rates of addiction, which in turn places a burden on local healthcare services. Additionally, the stigma associated with drug-related issues can exacerbate social isolation and undermine community cohesion. Families may find themselves caught in a cycle of despair, where addiction affects not only the individual but also their loved ones, leading to a breakdown in social support systems.

The security implications of drug trafficking in border communities are also significant. Increased drug-related violence and gang activity can transform neighbourhoods into conflict zones, prompting fear and anxiety among residents. As communities grapple with the effects of drug trafficking, the perception of safety diminishes, leading to a sense of vulnerability. This situation can create a vicious cycle where fear drives further isolation and disengagement from community life, making it even more challenging to address the underlying issues related to drug trafficking.

Ultimately, the impact of drugs on border communities underscores the interconnectedness of trade, security, and public health. While the flow of illicit drugs can often be used to justify stringent border policies or trade wars, it is essential to recognise that these measures may not address the root causes of the problem. Instead, a more nuanced approach that prioritises cooperation, community support, and comprehensive drug policy reform is necessary to mitigate the adverse effects of drug trafficking on border communities. By fostering understanding and collaboration, it is possible to create a safer and more resilient environment for those living in these vulnerable areas.

Policy responses to drug trafficking

Policy responses to drug trafficking have evolved significantly over the past few decades as governments recognise the complex interplay between trade, border security, and the illicit drug trade. Efforts to combat drug trafficking require a multi-faceted approach that not only addresses law enforcement but also considers economic implications and international cooperation. In the context of US-Canada relations, these policies must navigate the delicate balance between ensuring border security and fostering healthy trade relations.

One of the primary strategies employed by both the United States and Canada has been the enhancement of border security. Increased funding for border patrol agencies and the implementation of advanced technologies, such as biometric screening and surveillance drones, have been pivotal in detecting and intercepting drug smuggling operations. However, while these measures are essential for national security, they can also inadvertently strain trade relations. Heightened border security can lead to delays in the legitimate flow of goods, increasing costs for businesses and consumers on both sides of the border.

Moreover, international collaboration has become a cornerstone of policy responses to drug trafficking. Bilateral agreements between the US and Canada, such as the Beyond the Border Action Plan, aim to streamline security protocols while maintaining robust trade channels. These agreements emphasize intelligence sharing, joint operations, and harmonized regulations to tackle the drug trade effectively without compromising the economic benefits that stem from cross-border commerce. By working together, both nations can address the drug problem while minimizing disruptions to trade.

Another significant aspect of policy responses is the focus on addressing the root causes of drug trafficking. Both countries have recognized that reducing demand for illicit drugs is crucial in curbing trafficking activities. Initiatives aimed at education, prevention, and treatment for addiction have been prioritized alongside enforcement measures. By investing in public health approaches and community-based programs, the governments can reduce the need for illicit drugs, thereby decreasing the incentives for trafficking.

Finally, it is important to consider the economic repercussions of drug-related policies. Imposing heavy-handed punitive measures can have adverse effects on legitimate businesses and trade. Policymakers must strike a balance between enforcing drug laws and facilitating economic growth. Emphasising rehabilitation and harm reduction rather than solely focusing on criminalisation can lead to healthier communities and a more stable economic environment. This approach not only addresses the drug problem but also reinforces the notion that trade and security can coexist without leading to tensions or trade wars between the US and Canada.

Chapter 13: The flow of weapons across borders

The arms trade is a complex and multifaceted industry that plays a significant role in international relations, security, and economic dynamics. Understanding the arms trade requires a look into its historical context, the various actors involved, and the implications it has on global stability. This trade encompasses the legal and illegal transfer of weapons, military equipment, and related services, with countries engaging in both legitimate commerce and illicit dealings. The consequences of these trades extend beyond national borders, influencing conflicts, power balances, and, ultimately, the very nature of warfare itself.

In recent years, the arms trade has gained renewed attention due to its connection with global security challenges. The proliferation of arms often exacerbates conflicts, enabling both state and non-state actors to engage in violence. The rise of non-state actors, such as militant groups and organized crime syndicates, has transformed the landscape of the arms trade. These groups frequently resort to illicit means to procure weapons, undermining efforts to maintain peace and security. This creates a scenario where the legal arms trade, often justified by national defense needs, can inadvertently fuel illicit activities, further complicating the security environment.

The United States and Canada have established a robust framework for regulating arms trade through treaties, laws, and agreements aimed at preventing illegal arms transfers and ensuring responsible trade practices. However, the challenges posed by illegal border crossings and the flow of illicit drugs and weapons test this framework's effectiveness. The perception that these illicit activities justify escalating trade tensions between the two nations can obscure the need for cooperative solutions. Rather than allowing these challenges to drive a wedge between them, both countries must work together to address the root causes of these issues, focusing on comprehensive strategies that enhance security and promote stability.

Moreover, the arms trade is intricately linked to economic interests. Many industries depend on the production and sale of military equipment, which can create a conflict between national security concerns and economic motivations. Countries may prioritise economic gains over the potential consequences of arms proliferation. This dynamic is particularly relevant in the context of trade wars, where national policies may clash with the realities of the arms market. Understanding this relationship is essential for comprehending how trade policies can impact not only economic relations but also international security.

In conclusion, the complexities surrounding the arms trade necessitate a nuanced understanding of its implications for international relations and domestic policies. As illegal border crossings and the flow of illicit drugs and weapons continue to challenge both the United States and Canada, it becomes crucial to recognize that trade wars are not justified responses to these issues. Instead, fostering collaboration and addressing the underlying factors contributing to these challenges can create a more secure and stable environment for both nations. Through informed dialogue and cooperative efforts, the potential for a more peaceful coexistence can be realised, moving beyond the simplistic narratives that often dominate discussions about trade and security.

The connection between drugs and weapons

The connection between drugs and weapons has long been recognised as a critical issue within the context of illegal border crossings. The flow of illicit drugs often intertwines with the trafficking of weapons, creating a complex web of crime that transcends national borders. Drug cartels and organised crime syndicates frequently use firearms to protect their operations, enforce territorial control, and engage in violent confrontations with rival groups or law enforcement. This dynamic not only threatens public safety but also complicates border security efforts, as authorities struggle to interdict both drug and weapon smuggling.

In the United States and Canada, the geographic proximity of the two nations facilitates a significant volume of cross-border traffic, legal and illegal alike. While both countries have implemented measures to combat drug trafficking and arms smuggling, the sheer scale of these operations poses ongoing challenges. Law enforcement agencies often find themselves contending with sophisticated networks that exploit vulnerabilities in border security. The relationship between drug and weapon trafficking is particularly pronounced in areas where illicit trade routes have been established, making it crucial for policymakers to understand how these issues intersect.

While it is tempting for some policymakers to draw a direct correlation between the challenges posed by drug and weapon trafficking and the need for stringent trade policies, such an approach can be misguided. The complexities of the illegal trade should not serve as a justification for escalating trade wars that can harm legitimate economic interests. Instead, a more nuanced understanding of the interconnectedness of these issues can pave the way for collaborative strategies that prioritise law enforcement, diplomatic engagement, and community-based solutions, ultimately fostering safer and more prosperous border regions.

In conclusion, the connection between drugs and weapons is a multifaceted challenge that calls for informed responses rather than reactions driven by fear or misunderstanding. As the United States and Canada navigate their shared border, it is essential to recognise that effective solutions lie in cooperation and dialogue, rather than punitive trade measures. By focusing on comprehensive strategies that address the root causes of drug and weapon trafficking, both nations can work towards creating a more secure and equitable environment that benefits all citizens.

Legal frameworks governing arms trade

Various treaties and agreements aim to regulate the transfer of conventional weapons, ensuring that arms do not contribute to instability or conflict. The Arms Trade Treaty (ATT), adopted by the United Nations in 2013, is a cornerstone of this regulatory environment. It establishes common standards for the international trade of conventional arms, requiring signatory countries to assess the potential risks of their arms transfers and to prevent the export of weapons that could be used for human rights violations or exacerbate conflicts.

In addition to the ATT, several regional agreements play significant roles in governing arms trade. For instance, the Organization of American States (OAS) has established the Inter-American Convention against the Illicit Manufacturing of and Trafficking in Firearms, Ammunition, Explosives, and Other Related Materials. This convention aims to combat the illegal arms trade in the Americas by promoting cooperation among member states to strengthen their legal frameworks and enforcement mechanisms. Such regional efforts complement global initiatives, addressing the specific challenges posed by illicit arms trafficking and its links to organised crime and violence.

National laws also significantly impact the legal landscape of arms trade. Countries like the United States and Canada have established stringent regulations governing the export and import of military and dual-use technologies. In the U.S., the Arms Export Control Act (AECA) regulates defence exports, while the International Traffic in Arms Regulations (ITAR) outlines the procedures for exporting defence-related articles and services. Similarly, Canada adheres to the Export and Import Permits Act (EIPA), which mandates government oversight of arms exports to ensure compliance with international obligations. These national laws are designed to prevent the diversion of arms to unauthorised users and to promote responsible arms trade practices.

Despite the existence of these legal frameworks, challenges persist in their enforcement and compliance. The illicit arms trade continues to flourish, often facilitated by corrupt officials, weak governance, and inadequate regulatory mechanisms in various countries. This underground market poses significant risks, contributing to violence and destabilisation, particularly in conflict-prone regions. Moreover, the proliferation of small arms and light weapons exacerbates issues related to illegal border crossings and the flow of illicit drugs, creating a complex web of interrelated challenges that complicate efforts to regulate arms trade effectively.

The intersection of arms trade with issues like illegal border crossings and drug trafficking cannot be overlooked, as these elements often provide justification for heightened security measures and tensions between countries. However, it is critical to recognise that the existence of these challenges should not be used to justify trade wars, particularly between neighbouring countries like the United States and Canada. A collaborative approach that prioritises regulatory compliance, joint law enforcement efforts, and diplomatic dialogue is essential to addressing the root causes of illicit arms trade and fostering a more secure and stable international environment.

Chapter 14: Economic implications of trade wars

The impact on bilateral trade

The impact of bilateral trade between the United States and Canada has long been shaped by various factors, including economic policies, political relations, and societal concerns. However, the emergence of illegal border crossings and the flow of illicit drugs and weapons has introduced a complex dynamic that threatens to disrupt this vital trade relationship. As trade tensions escalate, it is crucial to examine how these illicit activities are perceived and the ramifications they have on legitimate trade practices.

Illegal border crossings have become a focal point of contention in discussions surrounding U.S.-Canada relations. While the vast majority of transactions occur legally and contribute positively to both economies, the presence of unauthorised crossings has led to increased scrutiny and suspicion. This atmosphere of distrust can result in heightened border security measures, which, while aimed at curbing illegal activities, can inadvertently stifle legitimate trade. Delays at border crossings and increased costs for businesses attempting to comply with stricter regulations can diminish the efficiency of trade flows, impacting both countries' economic health.

The flow of illicit drugs and weapons further complicates the landscape of bilateral trade. Concerns about drug trafficking and the smuggling of arms can provoke reactions that prioritize security over trade facilitation. In response to perceived threats, governments might implement policies that restrict trade or impose tariffs, under the guise of protecting national interests. Such measures can lead to retaliatory actions that escalate into full-blown trade wars, ultimately harming the economies of both nations and undermining the mutual benefits derived from robust trade agreements.

Both the United States and Canada rely heavily on each other for goods and services, with significant cross-border investments bolstering industries and creating jobs. The focus on illegal crossings and trafficking can distract policymakers from addressing the essential issues that sustain trade. By allowing fears of illicit activities to dictate trade policy, both countries risk undermining the foundational economic ties that have been built over decades.

It is essential to recognise that the issues of illegal border crossings and the flow of illicit drugs and weapons should not be used as justification for trade wars between the U.S. and Canada. Instead, cooperative approaches that address security concerns while maintaining open trade channels are crucial. By fostering dialogue and collaboration, both nations can work towards solutions that enhance border security without sacrificing the economic prosperity that stems from their bilateral trade relationship. A balanced perspective that acknowledges the complexities of these challenges can lead to more effective policies that benefit both countries in the long run.

Consequences for local economies

Border communities are uniquely positioned to benefit from cross-border trade, as they typically rely on the economic interdependence of both nations. However, the perception of security threats can lead to increased scrutiny and regulation, which stifles legitimate trade. When local businesses are caught in the crossfire of diplomatic disputes, they may experience a downturn in sales, affecting employment levels and overall economic health. The uncertainty surrounding border policies can discourage investment, leading to stagnation or even decline in local economies that thrive on trade and tourism.

Moreover, the focus on illicit activities often diverts attention and resources from the legitimate economic needs of border regions. Local governments may allocate funds to law enforcement and border security at the expense of community development projects, infrastructure improvements, and social services. This misallocation of resources can create a cycle of economic decline, where communities become increasingly reliant on federal assistance while their ability to generate local revenue diminishes. The long-term effects of this shift can be profound, as essential services and community initiatives suffer from lack of funding and support.

Additionally, the impact of trade wars can exacerbate existing inequalities within local economies. Smaller businesses, which often lack the financial resilience to withstand disruptions, may close their doors in the face of declining sales and increased operational costs. This consolidation of economic power can lead to a concentration of wealth and resources among larger corporations, further marginalizing local entrepreneurs. As local economies struggle, the social fabric of these communities can fray, leading to increased unemployment, crime, and social unrest.

The role of tariffs and trade agreements

Tariffs and trade agreements play a crucial role in shaping the economic relationships between countries, particularly between the United States and Canada. The imposition of tariffs can significantly alter trade dynamics, affecting not only the flow of goods but also the broader socio-economic landscape. When tariffs are introduced, they increase the cost of imported goods, which can lead to higher prices for consumers and potential retaliation from trading partners. This tit-for-tat response can escalate into trade wars, where both countries impose increasing tariffs on each other's products, ultimately harming their economies and disrupting established trade networks.

In the context of the U.S.-Canada relationship, the imposition of tariffs has often been justified by concerns related to national security, economic protectionism, and the need to combat illegal activities such as drug trafficking and arms smuggling. However, these justifications can overlook the complexities of border management and the multifaceted nature of illegal activities. Tariffs alone do not address the root causes of illicit trade; rather, they can complicate legitimate commerce and strain diplomatic relations. It is essential to recognise that the issues of illegal border crossings and the flow of illicit drugs and weapons are not inherently tied to trade agreements but are instead influenced by a myriad of factors, including socio-economic conditions, law enforcement practices, and international cooperation.

Trade agreements, such as the United States-Mexico-Canada Agreement (USMCA), aim to create a framework for free trade that benefits all parties involved. These agreements facilitate smoother trade by reducing or eliminating tariffs, thereby promoting economic growth and stability. However, when trade agreements are undermined by unilateral tariff increases, the intended benefits can be negated. The economic interdependence of the U.S. and Canada, which includes a vast network of supply chains, means that disruptions caused by tariffs can have far-reaching consequences. Increased costs and uncertainty can hinder investment and job creation, ultimately impacting the livelihoods of citizens on both sides of the border.

Moreover, the focus on tariffs and trade wars can divert attention from more effective strategies for combating illegal activities. Enhanced border security measures, intelligence sharing among law enforcement agencies, and community engagement are vital components of a comprehensive approach to addressing the challenges of illegal drug and weapon flows. By fostering strong bilateral cooperation and focusing on prevention rather than punitive measures, both countries can work together to tackle these issues without resorting to trade wars that could destabilise their economies.

In conclusion, while tariffs and trade agreements are significant tools for managing international trade relations, their role in addressing illegal border crossings and the flow of illicit drugs and weapons should not be overstated. Engaging in trade wars based on these concerns can ultimately do more harm than good, undermining the economic ties that bind the U.S. and Canada. A more nuanced understanding of the interplay between trade policy and border security is necessary to develop effective solutions that promote both economic prosperity and public safety.

Chapter 15: Diplomatic relations between the US and Canada

The historical context of diplomatic relations between the United States and Canada reveals a complex tapestry of cooperation and conflict, particularly concerning border management and trade policies. From the establishment of the Canada-U.S. border in the early 19th century to contemporary negotiations, each milestone reflects the evolving nature of bilateral relations. The signing of the Treaty of Ghent in 1814, which ended the War of 1812, marked a pivotal moment that laid the groundwork for peaceful coexistence and the prioritisation of diplomatic dialogue over military conflict. This treaty not only restored pre-war boundaries but also reinforced the importance of diplomacy in addressing border issues, setting a precedent for future resolutions.

The early 20th century saw the emergence of significant treaties aimed at managing cross-border trade and immigration. The 1909 Boundary Waters Treaty established a framework for the cooperative management of shared waterways, showcasing how both nations could work together to address mutual concerns. This period also witnessed the establishment of immigration policies that, while at times restrictive, emphasised the importance of legal crossings and the economic benefits of trade. These milestones underscored the potential for diplomacy to facilitate the flow of goods and people, contributing to the economic prosperity that both nations enjoyed.

As the global landscape shifted in the latter half of the 20th century, so too did the diplomatic focus between the U.S. and Canada. The signing of the Canada-United States Free Trade Agreement in 1988 marked a transformative moment in trade relations, leading to the North American Free Trade Agreement (NAFTA) in 1994. These agreements were designed to eliminate tariffs and promote trade, illustrating how diplomatic efforts can successfully address economic concerns. However, they also highlighted the challenges posed by illegal border crossings and the trafficking of drugs and weapons. While these issues necessitate robust security measures, they should not be used as a pretext for trade wars that could undermine the economic benefits derived from cooperation.

The post-9/11 era introduced new complexities into U.S.-Canada relations, particularly concerning border security and counter-terrorism measures. The implementation of the USA PATRIOT Act and subsequent security initiatives have led to increased scrutiny of cross-border movements. While these measures were instituted to protect national security, they have also strained trade relationships and created bottlenecks at the border. The diplomatic challenge lies in balancing security concerns with the need for efficient trade and travel, a task that requires ongoing dialogue and negotiation to ensure that both nations can address security threats without resorting to punitive trade measures.

Looking ahead, the future of U.S.-Canada relations will depend heavily on how both nations navigate the intertwined issues of border security, drug trafficking, and trade. Diplomatic milestones will continue to play a crucial role in shaping these interactions, as both countries must work together to find common ground. Addressing the root causes of illegal border crossings and the flow of illicit drugs requires cooperation, not conflict. By focusing on collaborative solutions and maintaining open lines of communication, the U.S. and Canada can uphold their longstanding partnership while effectively managing the challenges that arise from their shared border.

Current diplomatic challenges

The relationship between the United States and Canada has long been characterised by strong economic ties and shared values. However, recent diplomatic challenges have emerged, particularly in response to illegal border crossings and the flow of illicit drugs and weapons. These issues have sparked debates over national security and trade policies, leading to tensions that threaten the historically cooperative spirit between the two nations. Understanding these challenges is crucial to addressing the complexities of border management and the implications for trade agreements.

One of the primary challenges facing U.S.-Canada diplomacy is the increase in illegal border crossings. While both countries recognise the need for secure borders, the rise in migrants seeking refuge or better opportunities often leads to friction. The U.S. has, at times, responded with heightened border enforcement measures that may inadvertently affect legitimate trade flows. This creates a paradox where the pursuit of security undermines the economic cooperation that has been beneficial to both countries. Diplomatic discussions must focus on balancing security concerns with maintaining open trade routes essential for economic prosperity.

Similarly, the illicit drug trade poses a significant diplomatic hurdle. The opioid crisis, particularly in the United States, has prompted calls for more stringent border controls to prevent the trafficking of drugs from Canada. This has led to increased scrutiny of Canadian policies and has strained relations as the U.S. seeks more robust measures. However, such a focus on border enforcement can lead to a disproportionate response that may harm legitimate trade and economic interactions. Addressing the root causes of drug trafficking through collaborative efforts rather than punitive measures is essential for fostering a more effective diplomatic relationship.

The flow of illegal weapons further complicates the diplomatic landscape. The U.S. has expressed concerns over firearms crossing the border into Canada, often leading to calls for stricter regulations and enforcement. However, these measures can inadvertently create trade barriers and foster mistrust between the two nations. Diplomatic efforts should aim to develop joint strategies that address the illegal arms trade without compromising the flow of legitimate goods and services. This requires a cooperative approach that respects each country's sovereignty while recognising the interconnectedness of their economies.

To navigate these complex challenges, both nations must prioritise dialogue and collaboration. Engaging in meaningful discussions about border security, trade policies, and public safety can help to rebuild trust and strengthen diplomatic ties. Additionally, involving stakeholders from various sectors, including law enforcement, trade organisations, and community leaders, can provide a more comprehensive understanding of the issues at hand. By addressing the underlying factors contributing to illegal crossings and the illicit drug and weapons trade, the U.S. and Canada can work towards sustainable solutions that uphold their mutual interests without resorting to trade wars that risk the economic well-being of both nations.

The role of multilateral organisations

Multilateral organisations play a crucial role in addressing the complex issues surrounding border management, trade, and illicit activities such as drug and weapon trafficking. These organisations, which include entities like the United Nations, the World Trade Organization, and regional coalitions, provide platforms for dialogue, negotiation, and cooperation among nations. Their influence is particularly significant in shaping policies that govern international trade and security, which are often affected by illicit cross-border activities. By fostering collaboration, these organisations help member states develop cohesive strategies to counteract the challenges posed by organised crime and trade disputes.

One of the primary functions of multilateral organisations is to promote dialogue among countries experiencing tensions related to border issues. For example, the United Nations Office on Drugs and Crime (UNODC) facilitates discussions aimed at harmonising laws and practices related to drug enforcement and trafficking. This collaborative approach is essential for building mutual trust and understanding, particularly between countries like the United States and Canada. When nations work together through multilateral frameworks, they can more effectively combat the flow of illicit drugs and weapons, reducing the need for unilateral actions that could escalate trade wars.

Furthermore, multilateral organisations provide resources and expertise that help countries improve their border management practices. Initiatives supported by these organisations often include training programs, technical assistance, and the development of best practices for law enforcement agencies. By sharing knowledge and resources, countries can enhance their capacity to address illegal border crossings and trafficking. This cooperation is vital in ensuring that responses to these challenges do not lead to punitive measures that could harm legitimate trade relationships, particularly between close allies like the United States and Canada.

Chapter 16: Public perception and media representation

The influence of media on public opinion

The influence of media on public opinion is a critical factor in shaping perceptions related to border security, trade, and the flow of illicit activities such as drug and weapon trafficking. In the context of USA-Canada relations, the media plays a pivotal role in framing narratives that can either exacerbate or alleviate tensions between the two nations. The portrayal of illegal border crossings in the media often emphasises sensational stories, which can skew public understanding and lead to heightened fears about security and crime. This selective emphasis can create an environment where trade policies are influenced more by public anxiety than by factual realities.

Media coverage of drug trafficking and its associated violence often results in a distorted view of the issues at hand. Reports frequently highlight dramatic incidents, which can overshadow the complexities of drug trade dynamics and the socio-economic factors that contribute to these problems. The narrative that associates Canada with the influx of drugs into the United States is not only misleading but can also foster an unjustified perception of Canada as a threat. This misrepresentation complicates diplomatic efforts and can lead to calls for trade wars that do not reflect the actual collaborative spirit that has historically characterised U.S.-Canada relations.

Platforms such as Twitter and Facebook allow for rapid dissemination of information, but they also facilitate the spread of misinformation. Viral narratives can quickly shape public sentiment, often without the benefit of thorough fact-checking. When inflammatory stories about border security or drug trafficking gain traction, they can provoke fear and anger among the populace, prompting policymakers to respond in ways that may escalate tensions rather than resolve them. This digital landscape exacerbates the challenge of forming a reasoned public discourse around trade and security.

The framing of trade policy in light of media portrayals can lead to misguided decisions that overlook the benefits of cooperation between the United States and Canada. For instance, trade policies based on misconceptions about crime and security can result in tariffs and barriers that ultimately harm both economies. The interconnectedness of the two nations means that punitive measures in response to perceived threats can have far-reaching negative implications. By failing to differentiate between legitimate security concerns and media-induced hysteria, policymakers risk undermining the historical partnership that has benefited both countries.

In conclusion, the influence of media on public opinion regarding illegal border crossings, drug trafficking, and trade relations is profound and multifaceted. It is essential for audiences to critically assess media narratives and seek factual information to understand the complexities of these issues. Recognising the power of media framing can empower citizens to advocate for policies that prioritise collaboration over conflict. Ultimately, a more informed public can help foster a diplomatic approach to trade and security that aligns with the realities of U.S.-Canada relations, rather than the sensationalised narratives that often dominate the discourse.

Case studies of media coverage

Case studies of media coverage provide valuable insights into how narratives surrounding illegal border crossings, drug trafficking, and arms smuggling have influenced public perception and policy discussions between the United States and Canada. By examining specific instances of media reporting, we can identify patterns in how these issues are portrayed and the implications for bilateral trade relations. This analysis reveals that sensationalised media coverage often exacerbates tensions and fuels misconceptions, rather than fostering a nuanced understanding of the complexities involved.

One significant case study is the coverage surrounding the opioid crisis, which has been frequently linked to illegal drug trafficking across the U.S.-Canada border. Media outlets have often highlighted instances of fentanyl and other opioids being smuggled into the United States from Canada, painting a picture of an unregulated border that facilitates crime. This portrayal has led to calls for stricter border controls and has contributed to a narrative that positions Canada as complicit in the American drug crisis. However, a closer examination of the statistics shows that the majority of illicit drugs entering the U.S. originate from other sources, indicating that the media's focus on Canada is somewhat misplaced.

Another relevant example involves the portrayal of illegal border crossings by migrants seeking refuge in the United States. During periods of heightened migration, media coverage has often depicted these crossings in a manner that evokes fear and urgency. Headlines emphasising "crisis" and "invasion" have shaped public sentiment, prompting political leaders to respond with calls for trade sanctions or border militarisation. Such responses overlook the broader economic and humanitarian contexts of migration while framing Canada as part of the problem rather than acknowledging its role in providing refuge to those in need. The oversimplified narrative neglects the fact that migration patterns are influenced by a multitude of factors, including U.S. foreign policy and global economic conditions.

Additionally, the media's focus on arms trafficking has often led to misunderstandings about the flow of weapons between the two countries. Reports frequently highlight instances where firearms used in crimes in the U.S. are traced back to Canada. This coverage can create the impression that lax Canadian gun laws are directly responsible for violence in the U.S., further straining trade relations. However, research indicates that the vast majority of firearms used in crimes in the U.S. are sourced from domestic markets. This discrepancy between media representation and reality underscores the need for more responsible reporting that accurately reflects the complexities of cross-border issues.

In conclusion, the case studies of media coverage reveal how narratives surrounding illegal border crossings, drug trafficking, and arms smuggling can skew public perception and influence policy decisions. The sensationalised portrayal of these issues often leads to calls for trade wars and heightened border security, which ultimately fail to address the root causes of the problems at hand. A more balanced and informed media approach is essential for fostering constructive dialogue between the United States and Canada, allowing for collaborative solutions that prioritize public safety without unjustly vilifying either nation.

The role of social media in shaping narratives

Social media has transformed the landscape of communication, enabling individuals and organisations to share information rapidly across vast distances. In the context of trade, drug trafficking, and border diplomacy, social media platforms have become critical in shaping narratives surrounding these complex issues. The immediacy and reach of social media allow for the dissemination of information that can influence public perception, policy debates, and diplomatic relations between countries. The narratives constructed on these platforms often highlight the urgency of illegal border crossings and the flow of illicit drugs and weapons, which can skew public understanding and prompt disproportionate responses from governments.

The narratives propagated through social media often focus on sensational stories and anecdotal evidence, leading to a distorted view of the realities facing border regions. For instance, posts depicting the dangers of drug trafficking and illegal crossings can evoke fear and reinforce stereotypes about migrants and drug dealers. This framing can overshadow the more nuanced discussions about economic conditions, socioeconomic disparities, and the historical context of migration. As these narratives gain traction, they can contribute to a climate of distrust and hostility, complicating diplomatic relations and trade negotiations, especially between the United States and Canada.

Moreover, social media serves as a platform for advocacy and activism, allowing marginalised voices to challenge prevailing narratives. Grassroots organisations and activists leverage these platforms to highlight the human rights implications of trade wars and border enforcement policies. By sharing personal stories and statistics, they seek to shift the conversation from one focused solely on security and crime to one that includes economic justice and humanitarian considerations. This counter-narrative can create a more balanced public discourse, urging policymakers to consider the broader implications of their decisions on trade and border security.

Their endorsements or criticisms can significantly impact public opinion and, in turn, policy decisions. For example, when prominent figures advocate for a more compassionate approach to immigration and drug policy, it can challenge the prevailing fear-based narratives. Additionally, misinformation can spread rapidly through social media, complicating efforts to address the challenges posed by illegal border crossings and drug trafficking. The responsibility lies with both users and platforms to promote accurate information and engage in constructive dialogue.

In conclusion, the influence of social media on narratives related to trade, drugs, and diplomacy is profound. It has the potential to both amplify harmful stereotypes and facilitate more humane discussions about border policy. As the dialogue continues about the implications of illegal crossings and the illicit drug trade, it is crucial for public discourse to evolve beyond fear-driven narratives. A more informed and nuanced conversation can foster better understanding and cooperation between the United States and Canada, ultimately leading to more effective and just policies that address the complexities of these interconnected issues.

Chapter 17: Alternatives to trade wars

Collaborative approaches to border security

Collaborative approaches to border security emphasise the importance of cooperation between nations, especially between the United States and Canada. Both countries share a long and intricate border that is often considered one of the safest in the world due to its economic ties and mutual interests. However, the complexities of illegal border crossings and the flow of illicit drugs and weapons present challenges that require a shift from unilateral actions to joint strategies. By fostering collaboration, both nations can enhance their security while simultaneously supporting legitimate trade and travel.

One key aspect of collaborative border security is information sharing. The exchange of intelligence regarding potential threats can significantly enhance each country's ability to respond to criminal activities. This involves not only the sharing of data about drug trafficking routes and weapons smuggling but also insights into the methods used by traffickers and smugglers. By pooling resources and expertise, the U.S. and Canada can create a more comprehensive understanding of border-related issues, allowing for more effective law enforcement measures that target the root causes of these problems without resorting to trade wars or punitive measures.

Joint operations and task forces represent another effective collaborative method. These initiatives can include joint patrols, coordinated enforcement actions, and cross-border training programs for law enforcement personnel. Such efforts help to build trust and enhance the operational capabilities of both countries. By working together in real-time, authorities can respond more swiftly to incidents, which can deter criminal activities and reassure citizens and businesses on both sides of the border. This cooperative spirit can also facilitate smoother trade processes, allowing legitimate goods to flow without unnecessary delays or barriers.

Public engagement and community involvement are essential components of a successful collaborative border security approach. Both governments can benefit from educating citizens about the importance of secure borders while also emphasising the economic advantages of maintaining strong trade relations. Programs that encourage local communities to report suspicious activities can bolster security efforts. Moreover, involving stakeholders from various sectors, including business leaders and local government officials, can foster a shared sense of responsibility and investment in the security of the border.

Ultimately, the collaborative approaches to border security between the U.S. and Canada highlight the necessity of balancing security measures with the imperatives of trade and diplomacy. When both nations prioritise cooperation over confrontation, they can effectively combat the challenges posed by illegal border activities without resorting to trade wars. This not only protects citizens but also reinforces the economic ties that benefit both countries, ensuring that their borders remain secure while facilitating legitimate trade and fostering goodwill.

Strengthening bilateral trade agreements between the United States and Canada is crucial in addressing the myriad challenges that arise from illegal border crossings and the flow of illicit drugs and weapons. These issues, while significant, should not serve as a justification for trade wars that could harm both economies. Instead, a focus on enhancing trade agreements can provide a framework for cooperation, ensuring that both nations can effectively combat these challenges while promoting economic growth and stability.

One effective approach to strengthening bilateral trade agreements is through the inclusion of specific provisions that address security concerns. By integrating measures that enhance border security and facilitate the flow of legitimate goods and services, both countries can create a more resilient trading environment. Such provisions could involve the sharing of intelligence related to illicit activities, joint task forces for enforcement, and streamlined customs processes that prioritize legitimate trade while maintaining rigorous checks against smuggling and trafficking.

Moreover, fostering open communication channels between the U.S. and Canadian governments is essential. Regular dialogues among trade representatives, law enforcement agencies, and public health officials can help identify emerging threats and develop coordinated responses. This collaboration can extend beyond mere enforcement to include educational initiatives aimed at reducing demand for illicit drugs and addressing the root causes of illegal border crossings. By promoting awareness and understanding, both nations can work towards solutions that reduce illegal activities without resorting to punitive trade measures.

In addition to enhancing security provisions, bilateral agreements should prioritise economic interdependence. By recognising and reinforcing the benefits of trade, both countries can mitigate the negative impacts of illegal activities. For instance, supporting industries that create jobs and stimulate local economies can help reduce the allure of participating in illicit trade. Investment in cross-border infrastructure and technology can also improve trade efficiency, making it more difficult for illegal activities to thrive amidst legitimate commerce.

Ultimately, the focus on strengthening bilateral trade agreements must be rooted in mutual benefit and respect. The complexities of illegal border crossings and drug trafficking should not overshadow the economic ties that bind the U.S. and Canada. By working together to enhance trade agreements, both nations can tackle these challenges more effectively, fostering a cooperative relationship that prioritises trade and security without resorting to divisive trade wars.

Education and awareness campaigns play a vital role in addressing the root causes of drug abuse and trafficking. By providing communities with accurate information about the dangers of drug use and the impact of weapon proliferation, local organisations can help shift public perception and reduce stigma. Schools, community centres, and local media can serve as platforms for disseminating this information, ensuring that it reaches a broad audience. Additionally, programs aimed at youth engagement and empowerment can steer young people away from criminal activities, fostering a sense of purpose and belonging that diminishes their susceptibility to illicit influences. Finally, successful community-based solutions must prioritize continuous evaluation and adaptation. As the landscape of drug and weapon trafficking evolves, so too must the strategies employed to combat it. Local stakeholders should regularly assess the effectiveness of their initiatives, gathering feedback from community members and adjusting their approaches accordingly. This dynamic process ensures that solutions remain relevant and responsive to the changing needs of the community, ultimately leading to a more sustainable reduction in the flow of illicit drugs and weapons across borders. By focusing on community empowerment and collaboration, these strategies can address the underlying issues that contribute to illegal trade, proving that local solutions can indeed be powerful agents for change.

Chapter18: Summary of key findings

The analysis presented in "Unjustified Borders: Trade, Drugs, and Diplomacy" reveals several key findings that challenge the prevailing narratives surrounding the complexities of U.S.-Canada relations, particularly in the context of illegal border crossings and the flow of illicit drugs and weapons. One of the most significant findings indicates that the escalation of trade tensions between the two nations cannot be justified by the issues of border security and illegal activities alone. Instead, these factors are often manipulated to serve broader political and economic agendas that detract from the foundational trade relationships both countries have historically enjoyed.

The data collected throughout the research illustrates that illegal border crossings, while a concern, represent a small fraction of overall border activity. The vast majority of individuals crossing the U.S.-Canada border do so legally, contributing to the economic and social fabric of both nations. This finding underscores the importance of focusing on the legitimate exchanges that occur at the border rather than allowing fears stemming from illegal activities to dictate trade policies. Moreover, the narrative that illegal crossings pose a significant threat is often exaggerated and serves to divert attention from the cooperative efforts that have historically defined U.S.-Canada relations.

Another key finding highlights the role of illicit drug and weapon flows in shaping public perception of border security issues. The book illustrates that while drug trafficking and arms smuggling are serious problems, they are often utilised as focal points for broader political mobilisation rather than accurate reflections of the bilateral relationship. The rhetoric surrounding these issues can exacerbate tensions and lead to protectionist policies that ultimately harm both economies. Instead of fostering cooperation to address these challenges, the politicisation of border security can lead to detrimental trade wars that disrupt established economic ties.

Additionally, the relationship between trade and security is complex and requires nuanced understanding. The findings suggest that a more effective approach to addressing the challenges posed by illegal activities would involve enhanced cooperation between the U.S. and Canada, rather than punitive trade measures. Initiatives such as joint task forces and information sharing can lead to more effective outcomes in combating illegal border crossings, drug trafficking, and arms smuggling. By focusing on collaborative strategies, both nations can improve border security without jeopardising their economic partnership.

In conclusion, "Unjustified Borders: Trade, Drugs, and Diplomacy" presents compelling evidence that the ongoing trade wars between the U.S. and Canada are rooted in misperceptions and exaggerations surrounding border security issues. The key findings emphasise the necessity of distinguishing between legitimate trade concerns and the sensationalised narratives of illegal activities. Moving forward, fostering dialogue and collaboration will be essential in addressing these challenges while preserving the vital economic relationship that exists between the two countries.

Future directions for US-Canada relations

As the complexities of modern geopolitics evolve, the relationship between the United States and Canada faces both challenges and opportunities that could reshape its future. The ongoing concerns surrounding illegal border crossings, as well as the flow of illicit drugs and weapons, have the potential to strain relations between the two neighbours. However, it is crucial to recognise that these issues should not serve as the primary justification for initiating trade wars. Instead, a collaborative approach that prioritises mutual interests can pave the way for a more prosperous and secure bilateral relationship.

One potential direction for future US-Canada relations is the enhancement of joint security measures aimed at curbing illegal border activities. Both nations have a vested interest in maintaining border integrity, and by pooling resources and intelligence, they can develop more effective strategies to address smuggling and unauthorised crossings. Initiatives such as joint task forces and shared technology at border crossings can facilitate a more secure environment while allowing legitimate trade and travel to flourish. This cooperative stance can reduce tensions and foster a sense of partnership rather than conflict.

Furthermore, addressing the flow of illicit drugs and weapons requires a comprehensive strategy that extends beyond border enforcement. The two countries can benefit from coordinated efforts in drug prevention, treatment, and law enforcement. By sharing data and developing joint programs, the US and Canada can tackle the root causes of substance abuse and trafficking. This holistic approach not only enhances public safety but also strengthens the social fabric of both nations, demonstrating that cooperative policies yield greater results than unilateral actions or punitive measures.

Finally, public diplomacy will play a crucial role in shaping the future of US-Canada relations. Engaging citizens in dialogue about the benefits of collaboration and the dangers of isolationism can help build a stronger foundation for bilateral relations. Educational exchanges, cultural programs, and public awareness campaigns can promote understanding and goodwill between the two nations. By fostering a sense of shared identity and purpose, both governments can work together more effectively to address the pressing issues of the day, ensuring that the relationship remains robust and forward-looking. Both nations share the longest international border in the world, which has significant implications for trade, security, and cross-border relations. Diplomatic engagement plays a crucial role in managing these issues, allowing for constructive dialogue that can prevent misunderstandings and foster collaboration. Without diplomacy, the potential for escalated tensions and conflict increases, which could disrupt trade and negatively impact both economies.

Illegal border crossings and the flow of illicit drugs and weapons present challenges that require nuanced approaches. While these issues are often highlighted as justifications for punitive measures, such as trade wars or stricter border controls, a diplomatic approach encourages countries to work together to address the root causes. This may involve sharing intelligence, enhancing law enforcement cooperation, or engaging in joint initiatives that target trafficking networks. By focusing on collaboration rather than confrontation, both the U.S. and Canada can create a more effective strategy for tackling these challenges while maintaining their strong economic relationship.

Moreover, diplomacy allows for the establishment of frameworks that promote safe and legal migration. Addressing the factors that drive individuals to cross borders illegally—such as economic disparity, violence, and lack of opportunity—requires a comprehensive approach that goes beyond mere enforcement. Through diplomatic channels, the U.S. and Canada can collaborate on programs aimed at improving conditions in source countries, thereby reducing the pressure on individuals to migrate unlawfully. This proactive stance not only enhances border security but also bolsters the humanitarian aspect of migration.

Trade wars, fuelled by border issues, can have far-reaching consequences that extend beyond the immediate economic impacts. They can strain diplomatic relations and create an environment of distrust, making cooperation on border security more difficult. The imposition of tariffs or trade restrictions in response to border-related issues can provoke retaliatory measures, leading to a cycle of conflict that harms both nations. In contrast, diplomatic efforts focused on mutual benefit and understanding can help to mitigate these risks, ensuring that both countries can navigate their border issues without sacrificing their economic partnership.

In conclusion, effective diplomacy is essential in addressing border issues between the United States and Canada. By fostering open communication and collaboration, both nations can develop strategies that not only combat illegal activities but also enhance trade and economic stability. Rather than allowing border challenges to escalate into trade wars, a diplomatic approach encourages shared solutions that recognise the interconnectedness of both countries. In a world where borders are increasingly challenged, prioritising diplomacy is not just beneficial—it is imperative for ensuring a secure and prosperous future for both nations.

References

1. The Reciprocity Treaty of 1854 allowed for duty-free trade.
2. The Treaty of Paris in 1783, which ended the American Revolutionary War
3. North American Free Trade Agreement (NAFTA) in 1994. These agreements aimed to eliminate trade barriers
4. The Reciprocity Treaty of 1854 allowed for duty-free trade
5. North American Free Trade Agreement (NAFTA) in 1994. These agreements aimed to eliminate trade barriers
6. The establishment of the Ogdensburg Agreement in 1940 formalised cooperation on defence matters.
7. The Arms Trade Treaty (ATT), adopted by the United Nations in 2013
8. Organization of American States (OAS) has established the Inter-American Convention against the Illicit Manufacturing of and Trafficking in Firearms
9. Treaty of Ghent in 1814, which ended the War of 1812.
10. United Nations Office on Drugs and Crime (UNODC) facilitates discussions aimed at harmonising laws and practices related to drug enforcement and trafficking.

Also by DM Ole Kiminta

How the Western Democracies failed the world
Supporting Refugees in their Homelands
Dissuading Global War Mongers:
Dissuading war mongers
La Libération Monétaire en Afrique
Canada Post: Management failure to modernise mail systems
Canada Post management failure to modernise mail systems
Canada Post: Management failure to modernise mail systems
Live to be 200
Aim to live for 200
Aim to live to be 200
Western democracies failed the world economies
Wrong foot forward: US-Canada trade wars
Canada begs to differ: Never a 51st state of USA

About the Author

DM Ole Kiminta is a Canadian of Maasai heritage. He spent many years working in USA, Britain and in Canada. He is an Industrial engineer, Petroleum engineer and Chemical engineer. Ole Kiminta was educated in USA and United Kingdom. Some of his published research work include Material science, carbon fibres and other composite materials, Polymeric materials, and Particle technology. He currently works for the Canadian government and lives in Toronto Canada with his family.

www.ingramcontent.com/pod-product-compliance
Lightning Source LLC
LaVergne TN
LVHW090417210926
848480LV00002B/600
* 9 7 8 1 0 6 9 1 0 9 9 8 9 *